THE DUE DILIGENCE HANDBOOK
FOR COMMERCIAL REAL ESTATE

Reader Comments

Must Read if you are buying any commercial property. The author has done a great job identifying the items and issues that must be reviewed and considered before purchasing an investment property. The book takes a step by step approach and is very comprehensive. It provides good check lists and forms, and identifies many due diligence items that most people would not think of. I run a real estate investment company and would recommend this book to anyone who is considering buying an investment property.

— Mike Adler, President, Adler Realty Investments

The Due Diligence Plan Handbook for Commercial Real Estate is a welcome and pragmatic addition to the field of commercial real estate. It contains a step-by-step template for the due diligence process that can be utilized by both beginning real estate investors and seasoned professionals. I was especially impressed with chapters 4 through 6, which detail the inspections and reviews that should be undertaken to determine the physical and financial condition of the property. The information you will uncover through these inspections and reviews is critical to determining whether a property will be a good investment and establishing an appropriate purchase price based upon its physical condition and cash flow. Chapters 4 through 6 alone are worth the purchase price of the book. As an attorney I also appreciate the advice in chapter 3 regarding documenting all communications and developing a tracking system so that the buyer can make certain that all issues which have arisen in the course of the due diligence process are addressed. I highly recommend this book, especially to anyone who is new to commercial real estate investing.

— Charles P. Werner, Real Estate Attorney

If you're a broker, lender, buyer or seller in real estate, this is a must read. I'm glad to have come across this book recently and recommend it highly to anyone involved in real estate, commercial or residential. The Author did a fantastic job breaking down all aspects of what to look for when buying commercial real estate which can be also highly useful for sellers as well in preparing their properties for sale. The book gives you a very strong foundation in all areas of how commercial real estate works, leaving the reader with a very good overview of what to focus on prior to making the offer as well as during their 'free-look' period. I learned more reading this book than I learned in my college real estate courses. Easy read, well written and an excellent reference manual you'll want to keep on your desk going forward. Two thumbs up!

– Tim Hasselbach, Property Condition
Assessment Technician

Investigate Investment Real Estate Like a Seasoned Professional. What a helpful tool for anyone (including old pros) acquiring commercial real estate. Too many investors find trouble only after they have closed escrow. However, many after closing issues can be avoided with a thorough due diligence review prior to owning. Mr. Hennessey has provided a thorough overview of the items an investor should investigate. If the advice offered in this book is followed completely, even the most unsophisticated first-time buyer will appear to be a seasoned commercial acquisition expert.

– Bruce Blumenthal, V.P. Acquisitions, Blue Ridge Properties

Incredibly digestible and thorough!!! This book is fantastic. As a real estate attorney, I appreciate the concise pragmatic style in which complicated aspects of diligence are clearly conveyed. Diligence is an often overlooked component of real estate, and this book gives both the sophisticated investor and the first-time investor a playbook to focus on the important issues involved in a deal. I highly recommend this to anyone in the real estate business, as it will help refine your own practices.

– Brad Keyes, Real Estate Attorney

This information will give brokers another skill set and add tremendous value for their clients.

Investors are always looking for better ways and smarter team members to purchase investments with. This due diligence system helps you to become a more valuable team member.

– Mike Lipsey, President, The Lipsey Co,
International leader in training and consulting
for the commercial real estate industry

This book is well put together and easy to read. Plus, it isn't too big or too small. Plenty of real world suggestions and checklists which are great for everyone in any area of real estate; particularly Commercial, Industrial, and Multi-family. Even the folks in strictly single family residential could use many of the suggestions in the book to really help out their clients move through any given transaction and dispatch their obligation as a fiduciary.

– Todd Rubinstein, Real Estate Broker

THE DUE DILIGENCE HANDBOOK FOR COMMERCIAL REAL ESTATE

A Proven System to Save Time, Money, Headaches, and Create Value When Buying Commercial Real Estate

UPDATED THIRD EDITION

BY BRIAN HENNESSEY

Author of *The How to Add Value Handbook For Commercial Real Estate*

Printed in the United States of America
First Printing, 2018

ISBN-10: 1511996897
ISBN-13: 978-1511996891

Printed by Yajna Publications

Interior book design by Michelle M. White

Contents

Introduction

There's a huge problem in the commercial real estate business that nobody is talking about- DUE DILIGENCE. The majority of investors, real estate brokers and commercial real estate professionals barely scratch the surface conducting their due diligence when purchasing commercial real estate investments. Investors are taking unnecessary risks and throwing money away or making bad investments, by not properly performing due diligence. Brokers are putting themselves at risk for potential litigation and missing an opportunity to help their clients as a true ally by learning these principles.

Having and adhering to a proven system while conducting due diligence, allows you to do it faster, easier, more efficiently and you're less likely to miss something.

It reduces the stress; makes you feel more confident; makes the sellers and agents of the properties less likely to try to play games while negotiating with you. It ultimately helps to make you a better investor because you are more prepared to make an informed and intelligent decision to buy or NOT to buy.

Commercial real estate transactions are more complex than buying residential properties and have many more facets to the investment and negotiations. It's imperative you learn how to "deep dive" into the investigation of an opportunity so you can uncover those issues that can affect the investment, both positively and negatively. By learning how to do it correctly you will be in a better position to negotiate against any seller. You'll be armed and ready to strategically address those items and challenges to place yourself in an advantageous position.

This handbook was created to give an overview of the due diligence process. It is written in a concise pragmatic fashion as a real due diligence tool and is not intended as a voluminous textbook of information on the subject. It is based upon over 30 years of experience in the commercial real estate business and acquiring over 9 million square feet from private and institutional owners.

The fundamentals remain the same whether you're acquiring residential rental properties, an industrial building, a skyscraper or a retail shopping center.

Many of these lessons covered here were learned the hard way. There are two ways to learn; from your own mistakes or from other's mistakes. It's always easier and cheaper to learn from other's mistakes. I am convinced this handbook will be a useful tool from which investors can avoid mistakes in the due diligence process and gain a better understanding of the salient due diligence issues, as well as create value when purchasing investment properties. I say "convinced" because I wrote this handbook for myself over a six-year period of being an acquisition vice president for an investor and his investors purchasing properties across the U.S.

I decided after the first couple of transactions I did doing acquisitions, where I was taken to school and taught some expensive and humiliating lessons, that I was going to make sure that they did not have to be learned again. I simply "didn't know what I didn't know". So, I created a reference manual and system for myself that had all the issues that needed to be reviewed; the questions that had to be asked; the checklists I needed to go over, so that I didn't have to remember it all or forget anything. After sharing it with some friends, they told me that I should share it with others.

Eventually I put it on Amazon and was surprised by the amount of people who bought the book from all over the world and their responses. The book is #1 Bestseller on Amazon in commercial real estate books. I have seen it create a movement of sorts for many investors and real estate professionals who have realized the importance of learning the skillset of properly conducting due diligence when purchasing investment property. I'm amazed how far the book has reached to all parts of the globe. It's extremely gratifying to get emails and calls from people thanking and telling me how much the information I shared has helped them with their investing.

When I started doing seminars investors and real estate professionals were telling me that they were totally unaware of some of the things I was discussing; the questions as well as the potential issues and strategies I was sharing with them. Some of them had been in the commercial real estate business longer than I have been. This told me there was a huge need for this information. I've now made it my personal mission to share this knowledge and help as many people as possible with it.

It makes investors better prepared to make informed and intelligent decisions while investing in commercial properties. It helps commercial real estate professionals such as agents and property/asset managers to become more valuable team members to their clients, as they learn and practice these principles. They are separating and differentiating themselves from their competition because they are adding much more value to the acquisition process, giving themselves a Unique Selling Proposition. They're also minimizing the risk for potential litigation and optimizing value by getting more involved with the due diligence process.

The whole purpose of the due diligence process is to discover the potential problems with a property, reveal any hidden profit potential, and to verify all information that you have obtained.

In short, a thoughtful due diligence process will afford the buyer confidence that once the acquisition is complete and there will be no material surprises. It is vitally important that everyone on your due diligence team is on top of their particular assignment in the process and that communication lines are open to everyone on the team.

The due diligence process is only one aspect of the commercial real estate purchase transaction, but it is of fundamental importance. For beginning investors, this handbook will provide a useful and efficient resource to cutting through the minutia and focusing on the important issues as well as providing a number of cost savings and money-making tips. And for seasoned pros, there will be golden nuggets to help refine their due diligence practices as well as provide a proven framework in which to complete the examination. I still use it today as a reference guide while performing due diligence on investment properties, because we need reminding as much as we need learning.

I now have a video course teaching and expanding on the principles, tips and strategies. You can access it at: impactcoachingsystems.com/courses. In it I teach the "deep dive" skillset of conducting due diligence. Upon completion, you will be prepared to go up against any seller, for any property. More information on it is available at the back of this book.

– Brian Hennessey

Foreword

Thorough and thoughtful due diligence benefits everyone involved: Investors gain confidence, reduce expenses and avoid mistakes. Brokers save time and trouble and, more importantly, can elevate their client service. At the end of the day, a sound due diligence process creates tremendous value for everyone involved.

With this book, Brian Hennessey has encapsulated lessons from decades of experience in nearly every facet of the commercial real estate business. The result is an invaluable resource for reducing risk, maximizing value and accelerating the process of due diligence in commercial real estate transactions.

This book is a great tool that will allow both clients and professionals to leave the office earlier and sleep better at night.

– Doug Frye, Former President and CEO,
Global, Colliers International

Why You Want to Learn...
To Conduct Due Diligence When Buying Commercial Real Estate

Most investors who purchase commercial real estate super-ficially investigate and perform due diligence on the property and investment opportunity. By not knowing how to properly conduct a comprehensive due diligence process and system, they are leaving many times tens and hundreds of thousands of dollars on the table. This happens because they are unaware of: the questions to ask; the issues to look for; the hidden problems to try to uncover; and the most effective ways to turn these problems around so that they can be value creators and/or money savers.

Sometimes the best deals are the ones you don't do. If you are unaware of the problems and pitfalls that come with it, they become yours when you own it. That's why you want to discover as much of them as possible during the due diligence period of the purchase.

Some of the most common mistakes I see investors make are . . .
- Don't have a proven process or system they use to perform due diligence and therefore tasks are done haphazardly and important items fall through the cracks
- Lack of a definite tracking system to keep track of all the questions and issues that are addressed to the seller
- Not knowing where to look for hidden pitfalls in: the leases; financial review of books and records
- Not knowing what questions to ask of: the tenants; property manager; building engineer, brokers and

vendors, to uncover hidden gems of information on the property to use to their advantage

- Lack of proper direction and communications between all of the team members involved in the due diligence process
- Not knowing how to respond to the seller's push back on specific issues
- Not knowing the proper questions to ask and what to look for when analyzing the market where the property is located

There's nothing like experiencing that sinking feeling in the pit of your stomach when you realize that you forgot to ask that question or look specifically for that issue and now you own the property and the problem.

I can promise you that the seller of the property is not going to hand you a list of problems and issues, as well as all the potential pitfalls when you get under contract with them. All sellers are hoping you don't find any and will finalize the transaction, while many will try their best to steer you away from them. At the very least, they'll avoid giving you any ammunition to come after them for a discount or blow out of the transaction.

- In addition, you get at the end of this book . . .
- A Sample Lease Abstract Form (which shows you how to fill in all the salient deal points and provisions of a lease document).
- Due Diligence Checklist (a list of most all of which you should ask a seller for when negotiating a purchase).
- Due Diligence Document Checklist (A list of most all of the documents you should request from a seller when negotiating a purchase).
- Sample Tenant Questionnaire (a sample list of questions that you should ask of tenants when conducting a tenant interview).

This handbook will pay for itself many, many times over and will be a constant companion when purchasing commercial properties.

Top Ten Reasons Brokers Should Become Knowledgeable About Due Diligence

1. You become better equipped to help your clients when making purchase or selling decisions.

2. You set yourself apart from your competition. Most brokers are not familiar with the due diligence process.

3. You can help to determine if there are issues involved with a property that are unsolvable more quickly and you and your client can move on to more doable deals.

4. You will discover hidden problems that can be brought up sooner in order to find resolution before too much time, money and energy is spent.

5. You will prove to your clients that you are truly an active ally in the transaction by sifting through the information on the property to sort out any potential problems or issues.

6. You'll be better able to find potential value enhancers to increase the value of the property.

7. You'll be better able to discover money wasters and potential savings thereby creating increased value to the property.

8. You'll be better able to help your client navigate through the due diligence process and the entire transaction more smoothly and efficiently.

9. By becoming actively involved in the process you will be less likely to get involved with litigation based upon negligence, because you will be pointing out potential pitfalls and problems.

10. Your clients will see the additional value you bring as their broker to the transaction, which sets you apart from the rest; which will in turn ensure repeat business and referrals.

Some words to and for brokers after having been on both sides of the negotiating table:

The good news is the world of service providers today has had the playing field leveled with the advent of the Internet. It's also the unwelcome news. People's attention span has been severely curtailed and feel as though they already have all the information they need at their fingertips via the Internet. If and when you get their attention, you had better be ready to give them a compelling reason why they should be talking to you as opposed to one of your competitors. If you don't have a cogent reason for them to listen to you and grab their attention, you will be cut off, hung up on and forgotten in short order. This information and skillset is a huge Unique Selling Proposition and will separate you from your competitors with a "value-add" service 99% of them aren't even aware of.

The vast majority of commercial brokers don't know how to properly conduct due diligence, nor do they attempt to try to get involved. How do I know this? Because I was acting as a principal for six years buying a lot of properties (over 9 million square feet). I can count the times a broker assisted me with due diligence on my right hand and have a lot of fingers left over.

One of the hardest things for me to get used to when I first became an acquisition person was all the "broker bashing" talk I had to listen to. Mainly because I had been a broker for 18 years and it was part of my identity before going to the other side of the table. I found out fairly quickly why there was so much trash being spoken against brokers. They really didn't do much for their clients when it came to due diligence. I think that has a lot to do with the fact that they really aren't aware of what should be done. They "don't know what they don't know".

That is all beginning to change. We're starting to see successful brokers and their teams hiring "Due Diligence" experts to join as team members to offer up a valuable service to their clients. It's also a very smart move, because they will be less likely to get involved in litigation because they are actively involved in investigating the investment opportunity with them.

It's time for the real estate brokerage industry to "wake up" to the fact that unless and until they start being more proactive with helping their clients through the due diligence process and thorough investigation of the property they are helping them to purchase, they're running on the hope that they won't get sued and things will work out alright. Mean while the legal industry is targeting them regularly and winning in a consumer oriented, litigious society with an overabundance of attorneys ready, willing and able to take down those who still believe that "ignorance" is a defense.

I've got bad news for those of you who are under that false belief. If you get pulled into court and asked why you didn't help your client with the issue at hand, you best not tell the judge you weren't aware or knowledgeable about the problem. Because their next question will be, "Were you going to be compensated on this transaction?", and when you say to them "Yes, your Honor, I was.", you're going to hear something like, "Well then you should have pointed them to someone who did. You're supposed to be the expert in guiding them to avoid problems and issues. Therefore, you are responsible." You'll then be tapping into your errors and omissions insurance, which has some very large deductibles shortly thereafter.

Learning how to conduct due diligence is like learning anything else. The more you get involved with it, the faster the learning curve. I promise, your clients will love it and start looking at you as a more valuable team member. They will be referring you to others and making sure you're the one helping them to purchase their real estate investments. I know this because that's what happened to me when I got back into brokerage.

The world requires more value-add service from their providers. The future belongs to those individuals that understand this and provides it to them. By doing so, they will be getting more repeat business and referrals. It makes total sense to learn this value-added skillset and make it part of your program that you offer your clients. Many times, you'll be teaching these skills to your client and that will put you in a whole other light with them. Many brokers will say they help their clients with the due diligence process, but they are barely doing anything effective compared to what they should be doing.

For all the reasons outlined above, you want to make this a part of your value proposition that you bring to the table, which is a huge differentiator from your competition. It will pay for itself repeatedly. I teach brokers how to avoid potential litigation in my due diligence video course.

My video course offers a Certificate of Completion and a digital badge you can place on your LinkedIn account or other professional websites, upon a 70% or better pass-rate on the exam given at the completion of the course. You can find out more about it at www.impactcoachingsystems.com/courses and at the end of this book.

CHAPTER 1

During Negotiations of Purchase & Sale Agreement

Hopefully, you have chosen a detail oriented, deal making attorney (as opposed to a deal breaking one), that will help to resolve issues and work through problems creatively, as well as find and point out potential pitfalls. In other words, you don't want the deal breaking kind who will "have a problem for every solution". It is critically important that you and your attorney are constantly communicating and are on the same page. Also, you must feel comfortable and confident in their abilities to negotiate and focus on the critical issues (and to not waste time and money on immaterial issues).

If you haven't chosen a reputable real estate attorney, make sure that you do your due diligence on them before you choose them to represent you. Ask them for references, specific to the type of transaction you plan to be working on with them and about their experience. Having a good, competent attorney on your team can save you countless headaches and significant money. Do not skimp on this cost, because you do get what you pay for. Many times, you're better off hiring a senior attorney and paying more money per hour, than a less experienced, less expensive attorney, who will sometimes be learning on your dime, so to speak.

As you're negotiating the purchase and sale agreement (PSA) you want to have all the leases and operating expense statements (year to date as well as past three years) sent to you to start reviewing, if possible. Most often the seller is unwilling to hand these over until they have a signed agreement, but if you don't ask, the answer is always no. First and foremost, you want to see if there is anything in the leases that would prevent you from moving forward on the acquisition.

Review Leases and Create Lease Abstracts

- Look for any outstanding issues that may affect the leases such as: a cancellation/termination provision; buyout provision; a reduction of space provision; or any other issues that could impact the "value" of the lease. Immediately address any major issues with the seller or their broker to find out if they are aware of any information that could shed further light on the issue(s).

- Confront the outstanding lease issues immediately and try to resolve them so as to not spend unnecessary time on a transaction that has unsolvable problems and issues. Time is better spent on "doable" deals.

- Ask to review all tenant files and correspondence. This will give an indication as to what issues are going on in the building, i.e. HVAC, plumbing, security, etc. and which tenants you need to really be speaking with. The ones who are writing the current landlord will most likely be forthcoming when it comes to telling you what's "wrong" with the building. This will most likely be done during the time when you are at the building conducting the tenant interviews (discussed further in the book), after the purchase and sale agreement has been fully executed.

- When reviewing a lease document, be sure you are aware of and note in the lease abstracts* the following:

- Look for any rental concessions, i.e. free rent; beneficial occupancy (where tenant can occupy the space rent free for a certain period of time). Be aware of how rental abatements are granted in the lease, i.e. base rent and/ or plus operating expenses. Also note, in many cases, unused tenant improvement allowances can be applied as a rental credit. (You'll want to ask the seller for a credit for any free rent granted to the tenants that you will be obligated for to the tenants once you own the property. This must be requested and agreed to in writing from the seller prior to removing your contingencies during your due diligence period.)

- Tenant improvement dollars owed to tenant or landlord. (The same applies here with any tenant improvements owed the tenants that will be your obligation once you own the property. Make sure you have an agreement from the seller in writing that you will receive a credit at the close of escrow.)
- Renewal and/or expansion and/or contraction options (make note of any option terms in the lease abstract).
- Caps on operating expense pass-through.
- Fixed option(s) to renew rental rates (this could negatively impact the future value of the property).
- Property tax increase protection (Prop. 13 in California).
- Look for any operating expense exclusions that will impact the financial analysis negatively. For example, the simple exclusion of the word "property" before taxes could prevent you from collecting the overage amount of tax increases over the base year or at the very least make it difficult to collect and force you to consider litigation and all its uncertainties and costs.
- Early termination or cancellation provisions.
- Refurbishment allowances. (Again, if you're obligated to pay for this once you own the property, ask for the seller to credit you at the closing.)
- Special allowances for afterhours HVAC or electrical usage at no charge to tenant.
- Building hours (outside of the norm).
- Special computer room A/C requirements.
- Security requirements.
- Any other landlord expense that may be incurred.

- If the lease requires a "Lease Commencement Letter", be sure there is one executed by the tenant to verify commencement date; expiration date and rental increase dates.
- Confirm all the amendments are accounted for and that any changes from the original lease are understood and verified, if necessary, i.e. reduction of square footage; change of termination date; etc., and are fully executed.
- Verify all security deposits and/or letters of credit (and make sure they are transferred at the time of closing with proper signatures).

(*See a form lease abstract at the bac of this book in Exhibit A.)

Review All Service Contracts

Make sure you receive all the current service contracts that are in effect at the building including, but not limited to:

- Elevator Maintenance Contract
- Roof Maintenance Contract
- HVAC Maintenance Contract
- Interior Plant Maintenance Contract
- Landscape Maintenance
- Piped in Music Service Agreement
- Janitorial Service Contract
- Parking Company Contract
- Trash Removal Contract
- Property Management Contract
- Pest Control Service Agreement
- Hazardous Waste Removal Service
- Security Service Contract
- Metal & Stone Maintenance Service Contract
- Property Taxes Appeal / Property Tax Consultant
- Utilities Contract
- Union Contract (if there are any union contracts, make sure that you understand if they are to be continued, which will result in higher operating expenses, and the cost is accounted for in your underwriting).

Review carefully all service contracts in effect to make sure that they are cancelable with 30 or 60-days' notice. Make special note of any that is self-renewing for long terms such as one year or longer. If you come across any of these types of agreements make sure that the seller understands that he will be responsible for any costs incurred for early termination or be prepared to live with them for the duration of the remaining term.

You want to have the flexibility of bidding other outside vendors and replacing the old ones if you feel you can strike a better deal with another vendor.

Be sure to note any special type of needed service contract, e.g. roof maintenance to comply with the warranty.

Inventories

You need to get a list of inventories from the seller, i.e. lighting and janitorial supplies; office furniture, equipment and supplies; tools; spare parts; motors; building plans; desktop and laptop computers, etc. Retail properties may include seasonal decorations or other supplies.

Make sure this list is provided and included in the purchase and sale agreement.

During the due diligence process, you must verify that any equipment that is used as part of the operation of the property is listed, included and transferred at the close of escrow. Take photos of the inventory so that you can look to see if any of the equipment and/or supplies were moved out prior to the close of escrow. This happens often, especially when sellers have other properties in the area they own and can use them there.

Mechanical Systems

You need to address certain issues that you believe will impact the building from a physical, material or financial perspective that you discover with the third party investigative reports. You want to determine early on which items are going to be "deal breakers" and which ones you can negotiate on. Either way it's important to figure them out as soon as possible; and if possible bring them up while negotiating the purchase and sale agreement ("PSA") and make sure that the solutions to any issues negotiated are incorporated into the PSA so there are no "loose ends". Any items left out will likely be forgotten or "overlooked".

If that isn't possible or issues or problems are discovered later in the due diligence process, make sure you're aware of the costs involved and how it will impact the financial analysis and be prepared to confront the seller properly "armed" with the right information; estimates for repair or replacement, etc., as applicable, so you can legitimately ask for a discount.

Mechanical System Permits: Make sure that all permits required for the operation of the property i.e. elevators (annual and five-year load test); fire panel; fire/life safety; boiler; emergency generator, etc. are up to date and no outstanding violations exist.

I'd like to relate a quick story about how getting a head start can work in your favor. I was negotiating to buy a 150-unit apartment building in Colorado. As we were negotiating the purchase and sale agreement, I asked the seller's broker to find out if the seller would allow us to start the physical inspection at the same time. At first the seller responded with a 'no'. Then I told the broker that I was only in town for a couple of days and wanted to get a jump on the inspections. Besides, I would rather we both find out if there were any issues that were unresolvable before spending a bunch of money on legal fees negotiating our purchase and sale agreement. I told him I'd be happy to provide any indemnity or insurance coverage necessary to make him happy. He relented and said that would be fine.

The next day I met the contractors and all the folks involved with the inspections at the property. I spent time walking the buildings and meeting with the property managers, building engineers and leasing representative. About midday, the head inspector came to see me and said he needed to speak with me privately. We stepped outside and he told me they uncovered some structural issues that the seller had tried to cover up with plywood and mud, which he proceeded to show me. I asked him how extensive it was. He said he wouldn't know until they went through some more areas. I told him I was leaving for the airport in a couple hours, but to call me later when he finished up.

Later that afternoon, as I sat waiting to board my flight home, I received a call from him. He said he had finished his inspections and things didn't look good. I asked him to speak to me in in terms of dollar amounts. He then said he wasn't sure, but he thought the repairs for the structural corrections could run anywhere from $1.5-$3 million. That's all I needed to know. I knew the seller was not going to be open to that kind of discount, nor did I want to take on a project like that. I cancelled the escrow, thereby saving myself more time and money that I had already spent.

Lessons to be learned: "If you don't ask, the answer is always 'NO'." Also, sometimes the best deals—are the ones you DON'T do.

Choosing a Lender

Mortgage Brokers

You can choose to work with reputable mortgage brokers who come highly recommended. They will have a variety of lending institutions they work with, and will give you a number of choices that could work for your particular acquisition. It is best to let them know if you're planning to work with other brokers. Ask that they submit a list to you of the lenders they are planning on going to so there is no duplicity among the brokers you're using. It's best not to use more than a couple brokers at a time on a property, so that they don't step on each other with contacting the same lenders and create a lack of motivation due to excess competition.

Banks/Direct Lenders

You can also choose to go directly to a lending institution of your choice; either a bank, insurance company, credit union or other direct lenders. This could save you some money up front, i.e., loan points that would normally go to the mortgage broker. However, keep in mind that it doesn't always work that way, and you'll have to do your own shopping around and negotiating to make sure you're getting the best possible deal out there. A good mortgage broker knows how to work the lenders and create competition amongst them, in order to obtain the best pricing and terms for the loan.

CHAPTER 2

The Purchase & Sale Agreement is Executed

Third Party Reports

Environmental Reports

If there are any outstanding or alarming environmental or hazardous materials issues, you need to get resolution ASAP, i.e., a NFA "no further action required" letter from the local governing authority handling those issues.

Phase I Reports are basic reports that are done by physical inspection of the property, as well as review of historical records and aerials to determine if there are any environmental concerns or issues; if so, what recommendations are made. These can include lab samples collected to determine if asbestos or other contaminants are present.

Phase II Reports are done because of the recommendations made in the Phase I Report to further determine the extent of any suspected concerns, issues or findings. Also, ground borings could be recommended to pull soil samples, if there are suspected ground contaminants such as gasoline, petroleum products or tetracycline from a previous use of the property, for example, a gas station or dry cleaners.

Phase III Reports are the recommendations for the remediation and removal of any contaminants found as a result of conducting the Phase II investigation.

Property Condition Assessment (PCA) Report

If there is a report available, it will give you an idea of which issues were outstanding when the current owners purchased the property as well as what has been fixed or upgraded since their ownership. Depending upon the size, type and location of the property, as well as the Lender involved, you may be required to order one.

Due Diligence Resources and Companies

There are many companies out there that conduct due diligence and provide reports for the benefit of investors, lenders, insurance companies, etc. Depending upon your needs, available resources and scope of project, you may want to consider hiring one of the many reputable firms out there who specialize in conducting due diligence, such as EBI, AEI, etc. Be certain that you pick one that is on your lender's approved list before hiring them.

Seismic/PML (Probable Maximum Loss) Report

If available, it will indicate if the property is in an active seismic area and what, if any, damage was incurred in the last earthquake, as well as, what the probable maximum loss would be in the event of another strong earthquake. A PML of between 18 to 20 is acceptable to most lenders, over that creates cause for concern. This would be applicable to property located in California particularly.

Title Insurance Companies

I have been involved with a multitude of transactions over the years and have used a variety of title companies. Most will get the job done. You want to make sure that you are dealing with a title insurance company that will not only cover the policy more than adequately, but also will help you to work through the issues and stand by their service. I have consistently received excellent service from Fidelity National Title Insurance Company. They have worked through some very complicated transactions that I've been involved with and have always come through for me.

Other Reports

There are many other possible reports that could be generated, either as part of a report (such as the Property Condition Assessment Report), or as a totally individual specialized report; for example: structural, elevators, roof, air conditioning, ADA compliance, mold assessment, geological and any other aspect that could materially affect the property.

Ask for and review all available existing third-party reports that are in Seller's possession.

Ordering 3rd Party Reports

Make sure you bid them out to two or three companies who are approved by the lender (without lender approval you may be forced to have report completed again by another vendor acceptable to lender). Also, make sure that whoever you choose is aware of any issues that are of concern to you such as the elevators, HVAC, roof, etc. Let them know that you want them to pay special attention to those items you mention to them and to call you with their assessment of those issues when they are finished inspecting the property. This is important because there could be large expenses that will have to be dealt with once the property is bought and you want to be able to have the option of negotiating with the seller on those issues before your inspection period has expired and your money has gone "hard" (i.e. nonrefundable).

I'll tell you a quick story to illustrate this point. When purchasing an office building in Orlando, Florida, we discovered there were some sink hole issues that were being monitored professionally, after they had been corrected. When our lender required us to have a sonar scan of the property to determine the risks involved for further issues, we ordered a report from a reputable local firm who came highly recommended. When we turned it over to the lender they told us it was not on their approved vendor list, so they could not use it. I asked if we could get them on their "approved" list and was told there was not enough time left to do it. We had to hire an approved vendor off their list, at an additional cost of $7500, which we barely received in time.

Lesson learned: Make sure you get the lender's "approved vendor" list before ordering one of their required reports. Or, at the very least, ask if the vendor you're looking to use is on it, then make sure you confirm it in an email with them.

Loan Negotiations

When you have decided on which lender you're going with, they will send you a term sheet outlining the terms and conditions on which they will lend, i.e. subject to a minimum appraisal amount; debt coverage ratio; future financial hurdles; review and approval of borrower's financial statement, etc. You can be certain that this is just the beginning of negotiations for the final loan terms. Especially in today's lending world, you can plan on negotiating all aspects of the loan right up to the very end when they're about to fund. For whatever reason, this has become acceptable practice in today's lending environment.

Always take the approach that they are not the only lender out there, and you'd like to establish a business relationship with them to do more business, but not at any cost. Don't be afraid to negotiate the best possible terms and conditions for the loan. Always have an attorney who is competent in negotiating loan documents review the loan docs and to fight for your best interests regarding carve outs, guarantees, liabilities, indemnifications, etc.

There are many other terms and conditions of the loan that must be carefully negotiated, such as: reserves for tenant improvements; leasing commissions; capital improvements, financial reporting, etc.

*Be sure to have the attorney (and the mortgage broker, if one is involved) review the loan agreement and promissory note and compare it against the fully executed term sheet to make absolutely sure that the terms and conditions are the same and no changes or additional stipulations have been added that can come back to haunt you later. This is a crucial point because lenders will not cut you any slack when things start to go array; especially if the loan has been sold to another entity. They will refer to the loan agreement and note that was signed off by the borrower. If people were not paying attention while negotiating the terms and conditions, there will be a lot of finger pointing to no avail.

Better to have your attorney and mortgage broker scrutinize the paperwork BEFORE you sign. After reading it a number of times, it's easy to miss items that could have a negative effect later, should something go wrong.

An important note: Always try to negotiate a one-time assumption at no cost to the new buyer, especially if the loan has favorable terms. It won't cost you anything and it will enhance the assumption option for the buyer should they want to assume the loan and save money, usually one point of the loan balance.

Conducting Tenant Interviews

A crucial step in the due diligence process is the tenant interview. Most of the time the seller will insist upon having their representative present during all tenant interviews. If so, tell them you don't want the property manager there, because the tenants may feel intimidated, but if need be, you'll agree to their broker representative attending the interviews. It doesn't always work, but try your best to make that happen. There are many critical issues that can be found out about the building; its history and its current ownership, as well as, what improvements can be made to enhance tenant relations and retention.

It is best to have a tenant questionnaire (a sample letter is included in the back of this handbook in Exhibit D) sent to the tenants ahead of time to prepare for the interview.

(Obviously, you will want to modify the questions as they will pertain to the type of property you are looking to purchase.) This will allow them to think through some of the questions so that they may elaborate on them during your interview. It is important to find out if there are any outstanding issues that need to be resolved or any side agreements between the tenant and the landlord which may impact your purchase of the building. For example, "Does the landlord owe you any outstanding tenant improvement dollars or free rent?"; "Is there any litigation currently pending between you and the landlord now?"

Much can be uncovered during the interview regarding their tenancy and experience in the building, as well as the submarket area in general. Many tenants will give you a wealth of information, if you give them the right questions to respond to. For instance:

- "Tell me what your likes and dislikes are about this building."
- "Have you had any bad experiences in the building you can share?"
- "How is the security in the building and in the surrounding area?"
- "Have you had any problems with the HVAC or elevator?"
- "Have you experienced any leakage from the windows when it rains?"

These are some of the most important sources of information that you can tap into to learn more about the property.

Many times, I have heard things from tenants that spoke volumes of information to me about the property, surrounding area and ownership. More than a few times I had owners tell me that I knew more about the property than they did after they owned it for many years. That's because many of them never really have asked their tenants these types of questions.

Do not pass up the opportunity to interview the tenants.

It is too valuable of a source of information. It may even help to change your mind about going forward with the purchase. I've heard and witnessed disasters from investors who have proceeded to purchase properties after the seller refused to let them interview the tenant(s).

There are too many indicators to be derived from your interviews. For instance, you may go to interview a tenant in a large suite or unit, only to find out there are just a handful of people occupying the space. This will beg the questions, "How is business going for you?", "Do you need to occupy this amount of space?", "Is this your only location?", etc. You can also read the reactions from the interviewees, which will sometimes cue you to ask other illuminating questions that can shed light on valuable insights. Some of which the seller hopes you may not find out and continue with the closing of the sale.

In my Due Diligence video course, I conduct a mock tenant interview to demonstrate how to properly gather information from them. You can access the video course at: Impactcoachingsystems.com/courses.

Interviewing the Property Manager and Building Engineer

When interviewing the property manager and building engineer, keep in mind they are representing the seller and don't want to say anything that might upset the transaction. Try to get them to understand (if they're with a third-party management company) that if they're going to stay on with the building after the close of escrow, they're going to have to be forthcoming with information with you, "good, bad or ugly." This will sometimes prompt them into telling you more about the issues and problems of the property and tenants.

Interviewing the Current Leasing Brokers

When interviewing the current leasing brokers of the building, find out what transactions (if any) are in progress and what the salient deal points are on each of them. Ask to see any pending lease proposals, activity and transactions in progress reports. Ask them about what is happening in the submarket in terms of: activity, pending deals and tenants who are in the market or about to start looking for space that you may be able to go after, should you have the available space to offer them. Also, find out what recommendations they to improve the building or tenant relations. This will give you an indication as to how the current ownership handles the existing tenants and current leasing efforts. Let them know that you would consider keeping them on, but you want them to be completely candid with you regarding the current ownership's status with their tenants and the building issues (if any).

I will tell you about how I turned that question into a 26,000-square foot lease while we were in escrow during our due diligence period. We were purchasing a portfolio of office buildings. One of the buildings was 102,000 square feet with a full floor and some smaller suites available. While interviewing the current leasing brokers, I asked if there were any pending leases, or lease transactions or proposals they recently tried to make but were unable to. They told me that there was a tenant who needed a full floor they tried to make a deal with, but the current ownership wouldn't give them the tenant improvement allowance they wanted, so they passed on the deal. I asked them if they were still in the market for space. They said they believed they were. I told them to contact the broker representative and set up a meeting for me. I also assured them they'd be paid their standard fee if we could make the deal with them.

I met with the tenant's broker and told him we were in escrow to purchase the building and wanted to try to make the lease happen for his client. I told him I'd sign his commission agreement, which I did right there in his office. The we proceeded to work out the details of how I could structure the lease for his tenant. We ended up signing a lease during the due diligence period, (subject to us closing escrow, of course) which we did. The lender, and investors were all thrilled to have a sizeable lease completed upon the close of escrow.

Interviewing Prospective Leasing Brokers

It's important that you find out who the top leasing brokers are in the submarket that the property is located. Call on the top two or three brokers and ask to meet with them either in their offices or at the building, if possible. Find out what their impression is of: the building; where it fits in the submarket against the competition; what the competitive set is; what they think the building needs for enhancement purposes; what their impression is of trying to do deals with current ownership; what is going on in terms of transactions in the submarket; what tenants are looking for space; what the subject building can expect in lease terms, i.e. rental rates, tenant improvements, concessions, lease term, parking rates, brokerage commissions and incentives, and any other pertinent information that can be gathered.

This is your big opportunity to gather as much information as possible on the subject building's submarket, from the people who help drive the market. Make sure you are optimizing your opportunity to get as much information as possible. Ask as many questions as you can to thoroughly familiarize yourself with the building and submarket you're buying in. Ask if you can tour the competitive properties in the area with them, so that they can point out the strengths and weaknesses of the subject property against the competition, i.e. its competitive set. This will give you an excellent perspective on how prospective tenants could view the building your looking to purchase and how it stacks up against the competition.

Spend Time at the Property

There is much to be experienced and found out by spending time in and around the building and property.

You'll discover: what the tenants are like; how the parking works in terms of availability and peak hours; and what the surrounding area looks like in terms of activity and people, at contrasting times. It's important to check the property out at various times of the day to get a better feel for how it operates; e.g.: Is the HVAC running after normal business hours or on weekends when it's not supposed to? Is the building locked after normal hours or is the security for the building adequate? Is the lighting for the parking structure and around the property adequate and does it stay on 24/7 or does it operate at minimum standards after a certain hour, e.g., after 11PM?

Take time to discover any possible issues that could be occurring in and around the building such as: leakage from pipes, HVAC ducting, plumbing; cracks in the roofing, concrete, structure, glass; staining on carpeting, ceiling tiles, concrete; odors in and around common areas that could indicate the presence of mold or mildew; petroleum odor near the elevators, which could indicate leaking hydraulic fluid and any other peculiar smells that could indicate potential problems with the building.

You may be surprised at the different foot traffic that goes through the building. If the building is in a major metropolitan area, you may get some vagrants coming in the building when it first opens, using the restrooms to clean up. If located near a school you may get kids cutting through the parking structure or garage looking for a car with valuables in it. The point is that you want to be aware of what is going on in and around the building at various times of the day, in case there is a potential problem that you might not have known about, had you not investigated. If you don't, you may end up having to deal with problems and issues that you didn't count on or bargain for.

There was a property we were looking to purchase located next to a Gentlemen's Club. While it was in escrow we decided to go by it late one night because we had heard in some of the tenant interviews that there were some security issues in the garage with cars being broken into, due to late night activity in the club. What we found out was that in the garage after hours, it was an extension of the activities that were going on in the club next door. A lot of shady characters hanging out, while continuing to party in the parking structure. It colored our decision not to purchase the building. We would have never found out about it had we not visited the property at night. That's why it's important to visit the property at various times of the day.

Review of Books and Records

Review the operating expense statements for the past three years. You want to see if there are any varying trends in the building expenses, such as: electrical spikes in the expenses, thereby indicating perhaps a tenant may have increased their usage by adding many more employees or a night crew. If that were the case and you, as the landlord, were paying the electrical, you'd want to read this lease to see if it contained provisions to bill them for over-usage. You may even have the ability, per the lease, to put a separate electrical sub-meter in to bill them over and above normal business hours usage.

It is always helpful to have someone that is familiar with the type of property you're looking to purchase, to review the books and records. They will already have an idea of what the expenses should look like and if they seem like they're in line with what is typical. A property or asset manager will be able to quickly assess whether the numbers are in line, or off, so you know what questions you need answered. You will have to pay them to review the financials and books, unless you plan on hiring them to manage the property. In which case, you can try to work something out with them for their work involved.

This is discussed in further detail later in the book and in my due diligence video course in detail at impactcoachingsystems.com/courses.

CHAPTER 3

Other Critical Issues That Must Be Explored

Besides the issues discussed, there are other critical concerns that must be addressed in order to make sure there are no hidden "land mines" that will cause you problems after you've closed escrow. Some of these include: building and fire code violations not yet corrected; Americans with Disabilities Act (ADA) compliance issues; permitting issues; encroachments on to the property by adjacent structures, fences, etc.; pending litigation between the current landlord and existing tenants and other potential problems.

The following is a list of issues and concerns, that are by no means exhaustive, but does address many of them:

Documenting All Communications

It is super-important to note and imperative that all questions regarding ownership and the property or building, be put in writing and documented, i.e. *emailed*, with an ongoing list being monitored and checked on regularly. This is to make sure that no issue is overlooked or forgotten. This can't be over emphasized. If you're not doing that, things WILL fall through the cracks. I promise you. There are just too many things to remember.

Many owners, their representatives, property or asset managers will purposely put off answering or addressing issues that may impact the sale of the property, in hopes that you will forget about it, or come across another issue that may take its place, so they don't have to deal with it, if it's put off long enough. The fact that you have a response from them in writing, or have tried to address a particular issue, gives written confirmation that could be used later to your advantage in negotiations or, if need be, in court. At the very least, it will help to keep track of the many items and issues that come up during the due diligence process.

Develop a tracking list or process that allows you to follow up on issues and questions that you need addressed or answered. This will pay off later when the transaction progresses and people "conveniently" forget to respond to certain questions.

Before the end of your due diligence period (about 5-7 days) go through all your emails to see what has and has not been received that was promised. Also, check with your team members to see if they have any outstanding issues that have not been addressed or information not yet received. Now is the time to turn up the heat. If you're not diligent about this you will be in a less advantageous position to demand a response once your earnest money deposit is non-refundable at the expiration of the due diligence period.

If you do not stay on top of the issues, they will be overlooked.

Building and Fire Code Violations

There may be outstanding violations on the building that have yet to be rectified that the current owners aren't disclosing. It is necessary to go to the local municipal Building & Safety Department and check to see, if in fact, there are any violations currently on the property.

Make sure you also check to see if building permits and a certificate of occupancy (C of O) have been issued for the built-out suites. It's a good idea to get a copy of all the building permits and C of Os on file so that you have a record of them. If there are some suites/built-out units, whatever is applicable, that cannot be accounted for, ask the seller if they have the building permit and C of O on file. If not, ask them to check with the contractor who did the build-out to see if they have them. On larger suites or build-outs this could be a major problem with insurance companies if there were ever a claim and you could not produce the necessary paperwork. Ask the property or asset manager if there are any outstanding building violations that they have been notified of or have knowledge of that need to be addressed.

Be fully aware of what existing non-compliance items might be triggered due to tenant or capital improvement work. This could potentially turn out to be a very expensive oversight, should you not thoroughly investigate. For example, let's say you decide to remodel the common areas in a building, such as the hallways and lobby. Your architect or contractor goes down to the city building department to pull a permit. It is determined that the remodel exceeds a certain dollar amount and triggers the requirement of bring any common area ADA compliance for access, such as a handicap wheelchair lift or ramp. Also, the restrooms will have to be brought up to code. This could be a very expensive remodel. You want to know what the dollar amount or remodel event that happens which will trigger these required upgrades.

Making a trip down to the municipal Building & Safety Department can uncover all sorts of unknown or disclosed problems, issues or concerns. You definitely need to put it on your list of "Things to Do" during your investigation and due diligence of the property. Ask if there are any outstanding concerns or issues that may affect the property currently or in the near future, for example, fire sprinkler installation. Whether that be the re-zoning of the property or surrounding properties, future developments that they may know of in the planning stages, or anything else that may have a material effect.

Building Measurement Verification

There are many times a building may not have current 'as-built' architectural drawings or space plans, which helps to determine an accurate accounting of the actual square footage. Often a building's measurement numbers will be over or under estimated, depending upon who has owned the property and for how long.

It's possible that some additional square footage can be picked up if the building was never re-measured under the most recent Building Owners and Managers Association International (BOMA) standards. These measurement standards are published for all commercial property types. Either way, it's cheap insurance to have the building measured professionally so that there are no mistaken calculations on anyone's part. Later, when you go to sell the property, you can send them along to the buyer as your part of the due diligence materials as to the actual square footage of the building, which most times, will put them at ease that you had it professionally measured. It's an inexpensive and prudent exercise to avoid any legal complications later, and possibly save you a bunch of money upfront in the event the numbers have been grossly overstated.

At the very least, verify the square footage on the existing building plans to the current rent roll to see what discrepancy may exist. Compare load factors to existing tenant leases and any provided building measurement calculations, to see if there are any discrepancies. Also, confirm the actual load factor of the building to what it is quoted in the marketing of the building. It is common practice in many markets to artificially inflate or deflate the number according to what the competition quotes in order to stay competitive, mainly with office properties, since they generally have an add-on factor for common areas.

Walk Each and Every Suite/Unit/ Apartment (whichever is applicable)

Make sure during your due diligence process that you walk each and every unit listed on the rent roll for verification purposes. This will ensure that all the tenants and vacant units listed are accounted for and let you know which ones are actually occupied and which ones are "dark," i.e. vacated but still paying rent. By the way, most lenders will not give you credit for rent on tenants who are "dark". Also, you'll learn a lot about the tenants while you're touring their space, e.g.: How many employees they have? Are they filled or are there fewer employees in more space than they need? This may mean they are in trouble and/ or downsizing or leaving in the near future. Walking them can speak volumes to you, which will also shed light on the property and its tenants, that you can never get by just being told or asking questions.

You may also find out that the suite numbers on the rent roll do not match with the numbers on the doors, which could indicate a problem with overstating suites and square footages. At the very least, you will feel more comfortable knowing that all suites have been accounted for and there are no discrepancies, hopefully.

When purchasing a large portfolio of office properties, we were walking a large building with many tenants. We were walking all the suites and found that one of the suites which was listed as 3500 square feet, was missing. After walking around the floor a couple of times, I asked the property manager where the suite went. She said she didn't know, but would look into it. It turned out, the suites on both sides of it had expanded and took a portion of it. They forgot to take the suite number and square footage off the rent roll.

I found another suite of about 2000 square feet in the same building, that was listed as vacant, but was filled with boxes up to the ceiling. You could barely walk through it. I asked who the boxes belonged to. The property manager told me the tenant down the hall was temporarily storing them there, as a favor. When I asked how long they've been there, she said about 5-6 months.

I asked, "How are you supposed to show the suite to prospective tenants?"

She shrugged her shoulders and said, "I'm not sure." "Hopefully, they can get an idea from the floor plan we provide."

Not a good plan. I don't want my building running on the "hope" marketing strategy.

The other reason you want to walk them all is to see if the seller is trying to hide anything from you. After walking ALL the units in an apartment building, you may find that there are some that have mold issues; water or smoke damage; and have been cannibalized and used for "spare parts" such as cabinets, doors, appliances, etc.

Here's a good example of why you want to walk all the spaces: I was involved with the purchase of a large, full service hotel of 377 rooms, from a very well-known international hotel operator. They did not want me to see all the rooms because "it would be too difficult and inconvenient to the guests." I insisted we see them all. As I continued on during the due diligence period, I interviewed some vendors that had worked on the hotel. One of them told me that he believed there were many rooms out of service due to mold issues. I immediately called the seller and confronted them. I told them if they wouldn't let me see all the rooms, we would cancel the transaction. It turned out there were 55 rooms out of service due to mold infestation. We negotiated a $2.5 million-dollar reduction in price because of it.

You want to see it ALL, no matter how much work or inconvenience the seller may insist that it will cause. Once you own it, you own all the issues and problems that come with it. Proper due diligence will help you to minimize them. It usually raises a "red flag" with me when I hear sellers telling me there's no way they're going to let me walk all the spaces. If they are insistent, I will generally pass on the deal because I don't like to take unnecessary risks. I'll first ask them "What's there to hide?" and if they say "Nothing.", I'll say, "Then there shouldn't be a problem with walking all the spaces."

Insurance Issues

You should get a few insurance quotes on the property while doing your due diligence. If you don't already have a good insurance agent, see if you can get a good recommendation for one from someone you know and trust. You want an agent who has experience in insuring the type and size of property you're looking to acquire. Ask them about their background and experience as well as some references. In the event you need them to help you with a claim, you want to feel secure in the fact that they know what they're talking about and can be an ally for you when you must deal with your insurance carrier.

When it comes to insurance claims the trend seems to be for the insurance companies to find all the ways they can mitigate the pay out to their insured. That's why you need a good agent who will work hard for you when the going gets tough and make sure you're getting treated fairly. After all, they're the ones writing the business for the insurance company, so they don't necessarily want to alienate the agents who are writing business for them.

We owned five office buildings in Houston in 2008 when Hurricane Ike struck in September of that year. I was afraid to turn on CNN News to see what happened the next morning after it hit. Our property manager called to say that a few of the roofs were torn up and some fences went down. We also sustained some water and glass damage. When the insurance company came out to survey the damage they said they would get back to us in the next week or so. What they did was sent us a check for $250,000 to cover all the damage. The various contractors we had spoken to told us that it would take $1.3 to $1.7 million to repair. We told the insurance company that we were hoping to avoid litigation, but they left us no other choice. Our insurance agent got involved and helped us to get a settlement for $1.6 million. With her help and our persistence, we got our rightful amount. Be prepared to go the distance with the insurance companies. With the right help from the right people, you will get your fair settlement. The moral of the story is "Don't give up so easily."

Independent Claim Adjusters

If the claim is large enough you may want to consider hiring a private claims adjuster who will interface with the insurance company and argue the claim on your behalf. Usually they are former adjusters of insurance companies who understand the ins and outs of the business and can talk their language. They will normally use the same software programs that the insurance company uses to cost out repairs and replacements, so that there is no second guessing on your part. The insurance companies will generally offer a fraction of the settlement cost to see if you will accept it and move on.

Most people are not familiar with the process and will become discouraged and tired of dealing with them, so they accept the lower settlement amount without putting up the good fight to get what they deserve. The private adjusters will generally take a percentage of the increased amount over and above the original settlement amount, which is between 10%-15%. Well worth it, if the claim is sizeable enough. Once you get the private adjusters involved, the insurance companies take on a new demeanor, since they know there's no fooling anyone into settling for less.

CHAPTER 4

Energy Savings, Cost Cutting Tips & Other Items

Energy Audit

One of the more important issues that can have a major impact on your building expenses is its energy usage. Property taxes and utilities account for over a third of your operating expenses. It can be highly enlightening to find out why and where your utilities are running on the high side (if in fact there are indications that they are higher than normal by the cost and or usage).

For instance, you may discover that a major tenant in the building is using an extraordinary amount of energy due to running after hours HVAC or 24/7 crews that weren't initially agreed to in the beginning of their tenancies. Perhaps a tenant has added additional computer rooms that require more electrical and air conditioning that they didn't have initially when they moved in.

The type of lighting (for example T-12 vs. T-8 fluorescent fixtures) will use more power as well as various types of HVAC systems, depending upon the different configurations as well as age of system. LED lighting is becoming much more efficient and acceptable for standard usage in office, industrial and retail properties, as well as in common areas of multi-family residential. The switch over to LED lighting can have a huge effect on energy savings and will pay for itself in a relatively short period of time, depending upon the amount of usage.

It is definitely worth speaking with an energy consultant who can help educate you and show you where and how some savings could be accomplished. Many states now have energy benchmarking and compliance regulations that affect the current and future ownership of the property. It is important you understand what those are and how it can impact you financially, as well as the timing for your compliance.

An energy audit can help you to impact the bottom line in a positive way. Sometimes it can be as simple as installing timers or adjusting the start and stop times on the HVAC units. As energy prices continue to go up this will become an even greater concern that can "make or break" the cash flow of an investment. At a minimum, it will keep you apprised of the building's current electrical consumption status and allow you to plan how to better conserve utilities going forward. Energy conservation is an ongoing project in a building and one of the first areas that costs can get out of control quickly. By staying on top of it, you can keep your electrical expenses in check and benefit your bottom line profits, while adding value to your property.

Some of the simpler but effective conservation methods that can be used in order to conserve electrical usage are:
- Establishing guidelines for tenants and the janitorial service to turn off lights in the suites when they are not being used or after they've been cleaned.
- Educating the tenants as to how to conserve electricity and how they benefit by keeping expenses lower, will go far in keeping utility costs lower.
- Switching to lower voltage or less lighting when possible in some of the common areas.
- Placing light sensors in the restrooms and private offices and other rooms in suites so that the lights go off when no one is there.
- Minimizing exterior lighting, if possible, without compromising security concerns. For instance, landscape and parking area lighting.
- You'll find just by making some simple adjustments, a significant amount money can be saved, and will create additional value to the building by reducing expenses.

An Important Note: Depending upon which state you are purchasing property in, the utility contracts may be transferable. If so, make sure that the contract for the electricity stays with the property and not transferred by the seller (assuming the terms are more favorable than if you would have to go out and reproduce it the day of closing). This must be done while negotiating the Purchase and Sale Agreement and included as part of the contracts to be assumed by buyer, but no later than prior to removing your due diligence contingencies.

Some other areas that should be scrutinized for possible energy conservation are:

Parking Structure Lighting

Cutting out or down lighting in late evenings, i.e. 11pm to 5am, and shut off during daylight hours (weather permitting). Be aware of security issues when resetting times. If there are tenants who stay late or have 24 hour shifts, you don't want to compromise their security.

Tenant "bill backs" for Usage

Many leases have provisions allowing certain kilowatt usage per square foot, thereby determining just how much electrical usage is considered acceptable. If tenant's usage is suspect, then a meter can be installed, at their expense, and they can be billed back for any excess usage. If you don't have these provisions already in your standard lease form, make certain to include them for any future tenants and upon renewals of existing tenants.

Evaluation of HVAC Efficiencies

An evaluation of the HVAC system in a building will help to determine what types of energy savings can be achieved. For example, in a chilled water system it is important to make sure that the water temperature is cold enough so that maximum tonnage is being delivered throughout the building, thereby satisfying the building's needs more quickly and efficiently. Also, older systems that are coming to an end of their useful life, are huge energy users. Many states and municipal utilities offer incentives to replace them. You may want to consider looking into replacing an older unit as it ages and becomes more obsolete. The newer systems are much more energy efficient.

Eddy Current Test

This test helps to determine the integrity of the tubes within the HVAC chiller. Make sure that a recent test has been performed and obtain a copy for technical review.

Pneumatics

This is one of the largest potential problem issues in a building's HVAC system. Think of it as the veins in a body. If the system is experiencing major leaks or the air compressor is not functioning properly, or the air dryer is not functioning, thus causing the system to be corrupted with water, the building's HVAC system will run out of control. This could be an expensive problem in terms of energy savings and repairs.

EMS (Energy Management System)
a.k.a. BAS (Building Automation System)

The EMS system, which most buildings have installed, is in essence a "time clock" that also regulates the HVAC system and other building functions such as; lighting, locking and unlocking doors, etc. It is important to determine the age and functionality of the system and whether it could be considered obsolete, as well as the vendor support available. Is there a current maintenance agreement in place? Can the system be expanded? Will the license for the EMS system stay with the building? Who locally can provide repair and training to your employees? Can the system be accessed by website?

Insure that all passwords will be provided to you at the close of escrow. The password will allow the highest level of access to the entire system.

The newer systems are very sophisticated and perform many functions. You can actually monitor and adjust functions via a laptop computer or smart phone. Depending upon the size of your building and how many tenants you have, it may make sense to upgrade your EMS/BAS system to a more updated model. These newer systems allow you to run the building more efficiently, thereby saving energy and money.

There are now many software programs available that you can implement to automate and allow your tenants more autonomy, when it comes to accessing heating, ventilating and air conditioning (HVAC) use, as well as afterhours utilities. Most of the software programs now include auto-monitoring and billing, to streamline the property management aspect of it. This can be well-worth the expense to capture income that can otherwise go unmonitored or non-reimbursed.

CHAPTER 5

Mechanical/Physical Inspections

A few of the first places I ask to see when inspecting a property are the mechanical rooms such as: elevator equipment room; heating, ventilating and air conditioning (HVAC) rooms; storage areas and building engineer's office. Also, the roof is another key place to visit. I can usually tell very quickly how a building is being maintained by the way these various places are maintained; their cleanliness and orderliness, and how organized everything is. If I see things are in disarray, scattered haphazardly with trash, dirty equipment and old broken fixtures sitting around, there's an excellent chance that the building will have issues and equipment that are in disrepair and not properly maintained. Don't pass up the opportunity to look for these indicators when performing due diligence.

These are reliable "tell-tale" signs that trouble is lurking and needs to be uncovered. On the other hand, don't allow yourself to be misled by newly painted equipment and squeaky-clean equipment rooms. These may be a mask to hide some issues that are there, but hard to discern without a thorough inspection by a qualified contractor or vendor of whatever equipment you need a report on. Some sellers are very adept at steering you away from problems, so you don't want to get lulled into a false sense of security.

Remember, YOU DON'T WANT TO ASSUME ANYTHING.

Domestic Water Pumps

These provide water throughout the building. Make sure they are running smoothly and quietly and be aware of any rust on the equipment, platform, or piping leading in or out of the units. Rust will indicate deterioration of piping which will cause leaks or destroy the pipes.

Emergency Generator

The area surrounding the generator, as well as the generator itself, should be clean and well maintained. Look at the maintenance logs to make sure that they are up to date and that it's being started on a regular basis, i.e. twice monthly. An indication of not being run on a regular basis would be excessive black carbon around the exhaust. Have a discussion with the building engineer/maintenance personnel to find out more about the upkeep.

Check the log on the ATS (Automatic Transfer Switch) to determine that it is functional and being tested regularly.

Elevators

Check to see if the elevator's mechanicals have been modernized, i.e. solid state vs. relay switches.

Look at the elevator maintenance logs to see if they are checked regularly i.e., once per week and look for any repairs performed and/or repeat problems.

If cabling is stretched or frayed or digging into the drum, this will indicate a need for drum replacement. Also, if there is excessive carbon in and around the elevator mechanical equipment, this will indicate a lack of maintenance.

In addition, make note of the ride (Is it rough and/or jerky?) and leveling i.e. stopping at each floor even within the threshold, to determine whether maintenance and repairs are required.

Make sure that the One Year and Five-Year tests have been performed and ask to see a copy of the reports. This is required by the local building codes.

Hydraulic elevators are usually found in buildings under 6 stories. You'll want to go into the Elevator room, where the hydraulic fluid tank is located and see if there are any visible leaks or a strong odor of petroleum, i.e. hydraulic fluid, which could indicate a leak. Ask to see the maintenance log. Call the company who maintains it or who worked on it last. Ask to speak with the technician who worked on it. They will usually be able to fill in some information on the condition and remaining lifespan of the elevator unit(s).

Roof

Depending upon the age of the building and its locale, the roof can be a major expense if it needs replacing.

Visually inspect the roof to look for soft spots; stains and areas where the membrane material has pulled away from the roof surface. Also, look at the flashing (metal caps) affixed to the perimeter of the roof to see if it is pulled away, excessively dented or destroyed.

Be sure to look at ceiling tiles and/or hard lid ceilings on the floor directly below the roof for stains and/or wet spots. Ask the top floor tenant(s) if they have experienced any leaks.

A roof and mechanical inspection is demonstrated in my Due Diligence video course which can be accessed at impactcoachingsystems.com/courses.

Curtain Walls

Inquire about the curtain walls and ask if they have been re-sealed, if so, when and where, and if there have been any leaks. This can be found out through tenant interviews and interviewing building engineers and property management. Also, walk the perimeter of the building looking for corrosion of window sills.

Window System

An important question to ask during tenant and property management interviews is if there have been any window leaks. Check for new tiles next to the window system. This may be a mask for a water migration problem; especially on the top floor of the property. It may be a roof leak issue or a drain connection from the roof drainage system. In cold climates, the roof drains are insulated to prevent water condensing on the drain pipe due to warmer air surrounding the drain as it passes through the ceiling. Make note of the gasket system surrounding the window. Are the corners in each window tight or is there a void due to shrinkage? Look for telltale water stains on the wall below the window system. This would indicate water migration above or below the sill plate. From the outside, look to see if the entire color of the window system is the same. If not, the color disparity could be due to failure of the window coating. If the seller has had a window wet-seal completed recently, ask why. If only part of the property was sealed, ask if it was part of a multi-year project. Inquire if the warranty is still in effect and is it transferable to the new owner. Also, ask if the sheet glass is still in production and can it be purchased and delivered within a reasonable time frame. Make sure you ask for the vendor who handles the ordering of the exterior glass

Water Heaters

Inquire about the age and condition as well as physically inspect. Make note of any rust, corrosion or any leakage. Average age span id around 8-10 years. Check to see if there is a plate or sticker on it that tells when it was manufactured.

Fire Life/Safety Panel

Inquire about its age; are parts readily available? Is it up to code and when was its last inspection? (Get a copy of the report). Fire Life/Safety Panels reaching the end of their useful life can be one of the most expensive single items a new owner may be obligated to change due to the sale. Have the seller state, if possible, that the existing fire life/safety system is currently code compliant, and there is no agreement with any code enforcement entities that on sale there will be an upgrade required within a specified period.

Fiber Optics

If the building has fiber optics; are they owned by the building or by an outside company? The reason being, it is a potential income source for the building. Many times, especially with many tech oriented tenants, it's a huge selling point to say you have fiber optics access in the building. It can sometimes mean the difference between winning them over or not from your competition.

Fire Sprinkler System

If the building uses sprinklers, find out if they are on recall and if so, are they scheduled to be replaced. If the building does not use sprinklers, check to see if there are any ordinances requiring the installation of fire sprinklers by the local fire code. It is a good idea to find out if there are any pending code changes coming up in the near future that would impact you in the requiring of sprinklers in the building.

Electrical Panel Thermoscan

Thermoscan is the infrared scanning of the electrical panels within a building to determine if there is excess heat due to minor or major electrical problems or overloads in the building. Inquire when the last one was done and ask what the results were and obtain a copy of the report.

Restaurant Space

If the building has a restaurant space and/or Café/ Deli, visually inspect the kitchen for cleanliness (potential pest problems). Also, inspect the grease trap (if applicable) for proper maintenance i.e., cleanliness and no leakage.

Traveling odors can be cause for tenant grievances. Check to see if it is properly ventilated, or if they are potentially violating their lease provisions.

Building Entry Doors

Check to see that all building entry doors are operating smoothly and do not have excessive play.

CHAPTER 6

Physical and Mechanical Descriptions and Photos of Key Components to be Inspected

Here are some critical physical and mechanical components that should be looked at carefully while conducting your physical inspection

Not all of these components are going to be in every commercial property you come across. However, once you become familiar with these with their terms and issues, you will be able to look for and handle most any physical inspections, for all types of commercial properties. You'll also know more about the physical and mechanical aspects of commercial real estate than most commercial property owners and real estate professionals.

Chemical coupon rack with steel and copper sacrificial metal inserts

This odd looking plastic rack serves an important part for the condition and integrity of the internal piping chilled and condenser water in the property.

Water is passed over each of the metal coupons in this coupon rack to determine if erosion is eating away from each of the water side systems, each of the coupons have weight stamped on each, one for steel and one for copper.

At a predetermined time, each is removed from the rack and weighed to determine if the coupon has degraded in weight. This will determine if the chemical treatment contractor has protected the properties internal water side system.

Ask for the reports.

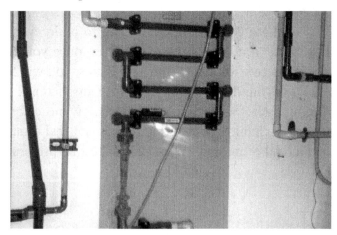

Condenser water bypass valve to cooling tower

This very important piping device will save the owner money in cold weather operation. Simply stated this valve will allow an amount of water to bypass the top or hot basin in the cooling tower to prevent colder water to enter the condenser side of the chiller. This valve will blend the water to reach an ideal design temperature.

The set points on this valve are critical to maintain the ideal entering condenser water to the chiller. The amount of water allowed to pass into the lower or cold basin will change depending on the outdoor temperature.

Ask for the set points from the seller.

Cooling tower tips (Photos 1-5)

Lower basin integrity can be easily determined if water is standing under the lower tower basin. Even with the preferred stainless-steel construction the bottom panels are bolted together with gaskets and sealant alike.

In the case of a two-cell tower there should be a gate between each of the two lower cells to allow draining of one cell to allow maintenance on the second cell.

If not, condenser water side will have to be shut down to affect any cleaning or repairs.

Determine if the engineer can easily access the top of the tower doors to perform motor maintenance when required.

Note screens to prevent birds from nesting under basin.

Elevator machine room temperature control

Elevator machine rooms are typically warm and have to maintain a set range of temperatures to protect the electronic circuit boards.

It would be an advantage to determine if the temperature control for the elevator machine rooms are served by a separate air-conditioning system.

If cooling is provided by the property's chilled water system it might add to the overall energy costs to produce the required temperature, rather than a separate air-to-air system.

Emergency Generator

Contained within each emergency generator's control panel or located on the body of the generator, you will find a run time meter called an hour meter that will show the amount of operational use for the generator.

- Record hours of run times, if original to property. Divide age of property into hours of run time to establish years of operational use. This information will allow the potential buyer to determine how often the gen-set was operated.

- Ask for the service records from the generator service provider to determine the frequency of maintenance.
- Ask if routine oil samples and analysis from the generator have taken as part of their property management program. Oil samples will show any copper and steel wear in the samples, and dilution of the generator oil will indicate possibility of fuel passing thru the injectors.
- Recent load bank testing at ½, ¾ and full load capacity. Indicate total amperage at each of the loads indicated.
- Test report indicating the time for the A.T.S (automatic transfer switch) transfer from commercial power to emergency transfer. Then reverse transfer after commercial power is restored.
- Record the run time to allow the generator cool down cycle to complete.
- Ask for the records for the generator battery service and load testing for deep cycle capacity.
- A true emergency generator is a standalone entity, not depending to be supplied by an additional source of any kind to perform its critical task, Example: thermostat controlled fresh water dump not requiring an engine mounted radiator, remotely located radiator and fan system to exhaust the hot air.
- Self contained approved fuel storage tank for at least an 8 hour run time at full load capacity.
- Emergency fuel supplier and generator maintenance contractor information located on control panel of engine.
- Ask if any of the existing tenants have been allowed to use or been connected to the building generator. This can be a real risk to both the new owner and tenant alike. Ask for them to provide documents authorizing their use, it if this has been allowed.

Improvements invested in the mechanical infrastructure

Pay close attention to added or replaced components in the mechanical systems.

As an example:

This owner has replaced both of the back-check valves, valves as these do not close completely over time due to wear, this owner removed and replaced with new improved valves as a matter of good practices.

New air compressor in fire pump room for dry system to detached garage.

New 4 ton split air-conditioning system condensing unit for service elevator equipment room.

New motors on domestic pump and replacement motors on domestic water system.

Chiller improvements by owner.

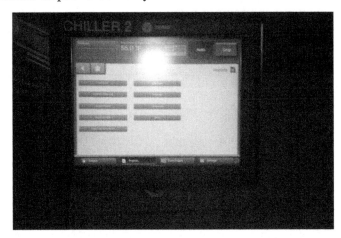

Replacement of control panels on both chillers with Direct Digital Control allowing owner to program and control chillers off site.

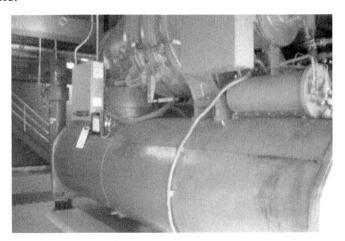

Roof inspection tips

Even after a new and expensive roof has been installed there can be damage to elements contained within the new system.

Workers that clean the windows, will in many instances, use rope fastening devices to allow support from the buildings parapet wall. These can and will damage or puncture the flashing that protects the side wall from water infiltration, more commonly known as the cant flashing.

Expansion joint sealant will degrade from Ultra Violet light and breakdown after several years. Membrane covering the entire vertical surface and run up under the coping flashing is the best protection.

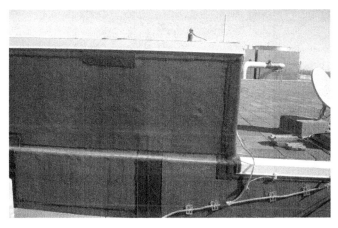

Tips regarding Loading Dock Evaluation

Does the loading dock have sufficient space to allow large trucks to maneuver to unload materials?

Will smaller trucks have to be used to allow new tenants to move in to the property?

Does the height of the docks allow for high trailers and lower trucks allow space for construction dumpsters and or trash containers?

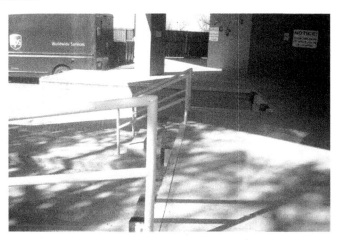

Air Quality Issues

Is there a fresh air intake located near the loading dock that would allow truck exhaust to enter building?

Vertical Transportation tips for consideration

First appearance when evaluating the properties vertical transportation system could be as simple as the cleanliness of the machine rooms as a starting place.

Housekeeping in these rooms can indicate the level of attention by the contractor.

If possible, have the elevator contractor lift several cabs to inspect the elevator pit below to determine if maintenance is being completed.

Were the elevators upgraded, overlaid, or other descriptions used to show improvements in the system?

By visual inspection do the cables or ropes show any rust color fine powder or rouging. Are there any strands showing on the steel cable?

If modernized, is the new system proprietary to one manu-facture to service or not? Can the new system be serviced by other contractors?

Many times, the modernization contractor will specify that they will retain ownership of a "TOOL" that will prevent a out-side maintenance contractor from servicing the system.

All testing reports should be available for personnel review, yearly and 5 year inspections alike.

Are temperatures in each of the machine rooms within the desired limits to prevent damage to the electronic circuit boards?

Window washing Davit bases and arm certifications

One of the most commonly overlooked systems during a property inspection is the roof mounted davits and arms.

Current OSHA requirements dictate that the davit bases be tested to support a working load in all directions.

Many window washing contractors will require a certification indicating testing of the bases and arms have been completed before use from the building owner.

This also includes rope decent systems. (RDS)

Prospective property buyer could be unaware of any failures in these systems unless provided with a current certification of compliance from an approved testing agency.

CHAPTER 7

Review of Property's Books and Records

Property Documents

The value of having the building 'as-built' building plans cannot be underestimated to the prospective buyer. Not having these on-site to reference will cause loss of valuable time needed to operate the new property. Mechanical, electrical, plumbing and all design data are contained within the as-builts. If the seller indicates that they are unaware of their location, have the seller inquire with the city building department if the set of permit drawings are on file, and have them get a copy.

The property's project manual is as valuable as the as-builts. This book contains all of the sections required to construct the building and it will give you insight to the level of detail that the design team used to create the site. Within the manual will be specific levels of information such as: elevator speeds; chiller tonnage; live and dead load floor loading, etc. Not all properties have a project manual, but the larger ones generally will.

In addition, operating and maintenance manuals would include the submittals that were provided by the vendors during construction. Most of the equipment will not be in the warranty period, but will provide valuable information to you as a new owner of the building: specifications; recommended maintenance, etc.

Review of Operating Expenses

You want to get at least the last two to three years' operating expense history/reports on the building, as well as year to date. This will not only show you what and how the expenses are, but also, any trends that may be occurring such as electrical usage, elevator and/or HVAC repairs, continuous maintenance issues, i.e. roof repairs; plumbing issues, etc. It will also indicate where you can implement cost cutting measures which go straight to the "bottom line."

What you're looking for are the "red flags" that point to recurring problems and expenses so you can pay special attention in investigating those issues.

Always ask for copies of all the utility bills for at least the past two years.

Be sure to question any large amounts and ask for detailed back up information to determine where the money is being spent. It could be a buried association fee or maintenance expense; an energy conservation agreement, which includes the financing of the equipment; roof maintenance contract required by the installer, etc.

If you're not familiar with the area and property type, try to benchmark the expenses against comparable properties in the area so you determine if the expenses are in line. One way to find out is to talk to some property management companies in the area, as well as commercial brokers who handle similar properties. This is a worthwhile exercise because it will help you in determining if you're on track with the expenses you're using, or if they're too high, you need to know what has to be done to bring them more in line.

An Important Note: Make sure you compare the operating expenses provided by ownership to the Offering Memorandum and financial/Argus Run provided by the brokerage firm, if available, to see if there are any discrepancies and/or missing information. This can impact your underwriting significantly, if you're not careful.

Ask for back up information, such as receipts; work orders; certificates of completion (if necessary); anything that helps you to better understand what has been performed so that you can satisfy yourself as to whether the issues have been addressed or just "band-aids" applied to take the cheapest way out.

Don't be afraid to ask the tough questions and don't assume anything. When in doubt, ask. You need to know all the answers to fully understand what has been done in the building and/or what needs to be addressed. This could have a major negative impact on the investment.

As a reminder, always ask the questions through e-mail so you have documentation of the answers and can keep track of the questions asked.

An Important Note: Call the contractors who performed the work on the repairs and maintenance at the property as well as current vendors who perform routine maintenance, such as HVAC and elevators. Ask them if there are any problems or issues that they can shed light on for you. You'd be surprised how much information they're willing to share. I have uncovered many issues and problems that would not have necessarily been discovered had I not had a conversation with some of them. They want you to continue to do business with them once you own the property, so many times they will be forthcoming with information that is extremely helpful.

CAM (Common Area Maintenance) Reconciliations

The CAM reconciliations are an important component of the property's financials. These are expense recoveries paid by the tenant based upon their base year expense stop or other terms in their lease, e.g., after hours HVAC costs; extraordinary electrical usage over and above normal usage. These are primarily for office and retail properties, but are sometimes used in industrial as well.

Base Year Expenses

The base year is the first year the lease is in effect or some-times the calendar year the lease is signed. This is typically used in a full service gross or modified gross basis lease document, where the Landlord pays the majority of the expenses, such as office properties. It determines the amount of expenses that it costs the owner to run the property. For example, let's say a tenant signs a five-year lease, full service gross lease for 5,000 square feet in a 50,000 square foot office building. If the build-ing costs the owner $12.00 per square foot to run annually for all the expenses, such as property taxes, insurance, maintenance, janitorial, utilities, etc., that will be the base year amount that is applied to the lease. Let's say the following year the owner's expenses go up 3%, or to $12.36 per square foot. If the tenant occupies 10% of the building, they will pay their pro-rated share of the expenses based upon the differential of 36 cents. If the expenses go up again an additional 5% the next year, they will pay their pro-rata share of the increases in expenses over and above the $12.00 per square foot base year expenses, until the lease expires. If they renew their lease there, they can ask for a new base year, with the first year of the new lease determining the base year amount expense.

If you are running your financial analysis and basing the property's income on CAM pass-throughs, you need to under-stand how they are passed through and exactly to each tenant, as per their lease document. For example, if a large tenant in the building is at the end of their ten-year lease, their pass-through amount (the amount passed through to the tenant) most likely will disappear, assuming they remain in the building and re-new, because they will get a new base year when the new term starts. Make sure you get a copy of the previous two year's CAM reconciliation reports to verify CAM income and to ensure that you can do CAM reconciliations going forward. In addition, re-quest history for all of the Operating Expense Base Year informa-tion. After the escrow is closed, your tenants might ask you for information on how their Base Year was calculated. You need to be able to explain that to them and provide backup facts.

Also, upon the close of escrow, you want to make sure that you're receiving the proper credit for any CAMs that have been prepaid or credited to a tenant, although there is usually a time frame negotiated in the purchase and sale agreement for the reconciliation of CAM differential between buyer and seller. You want to get as much information as possible to minimize having to chase them down to collect your money after escrow closes, which is always more difficult.

Aging Report

Ask for a copy of the most recent aging report, which shows the tenants who are current with their payments and which ones are behind (including how much is owed); what categories do they owe on, such as rent, pass-throughs of operating expenses, special expenses incurred, etc., and how long they've been behind, i.e. 30, 60, 90 days, etc.

The Aging Report will tell you a lot about who is a chronic late payer or who you can expect to have a problem with. Ask the property manager if there are any tenants who are habitually late in rent payments. They won't always tell you the truth, but you can get an idea from the Aging Report. Also, when reviewing the tenant files for correspondence, you will see late notices which will "red flag" those tenants who are late payers.

Question all delinquent rents. Many insights on charges can come from the review of the delinquent rent. Delinquent rent many times is caused by tenant dispute of the charges. If the charges were not collectable, they would ultimately affect the proforma of the building. When interviewing a tenant who has a history of late paying or disputes, dig deeper by asking them why. You may be surprised by what they will tell you and their explanations.

Get a detailed report for each tenant to determine what the delinquency consists of specifically and if any amounts are being disputed. Also, prepaid rent or any credits owed to the tenants should be reflected in the report and buyer should receive a credit.

Warranties

Make sure you get copies of all the existing warranties on the property e.g., equipment, roof, etc. and make sure they are transferable. This could easily fall through the cracks if not addressed. These are too valuable to overlook and can be very difficult to get after the transaction is completed. Many sellers purge all their records and related documents on a property once they dispose of it.

Parking

Be certain the property meets the local city code requirements in terms of adequate parking ratios and handicap parking spaces needed. Also, when reviewing leases, verify there are enough parking spaces to accommodate the unleased square footage currently available in the building. For example, the landlord may have oversold the parking to lease space to a tenant with excessive parking needs, thereby leaving less for the remaining space to be leased. This is generally fine, if it does not exceed 1.25 times the allocated parking ratio.

Parking has become a very important issue as the amount of square footage allocated to employees for many companies has decreased over the years. The trend is to get more people in less space. Many companies have implemented collaborative work spaces with open areas which are predominant in their office space, which allows for more people in less square footage. Having more parking spaces can mean the difference of you getting the tenant or not, if your building is under parked. Many times, a building that has an abundance of parking will win the tenant solely because they can accommodate their parking needs.

Interview the current parking lot operator, if it is operated by a third-party vendor. Make sure that the contract is cancelable. If not, you want to try and negotiate with the seller for picking up the difference in savings you could have had by switching to another operator. At the very least have them pay for the cancellation penalty.

A current trend in parking garages is to automate them, which reduces expenses considerably and goes right to the bottom line. It will usually pay for itself within a couple of years and then becomes pure profit. It is worth looking into if your building is large enough to warrant it. Ask a reliable third-party parking company that handles automated systems to give you a proposal. It will explain the costs, as well as the estimated payback time.

During tenant interviews, ask tenants if they find the parking availability to be adequate and if there are any suggestions or issues they would like to address.

Ground Leases

In the event there is a ground lease involved in the purchase of a building, it is imperative you understand all aspects, costs and requirements as the ground lessee and how it impacts your financial analysis. Make certain that you allow enough time to get an estoppel certificate signed by the ground lessor.

Dealing with ground leases always requires more time than projected. Be sure to allow ample time to deal with a ground lease scenario. It is similar to conducting a whole other transaction in itself, only you're dealing with a somewhat disinterested third party or parties when the ground lessor has nothing to derive.

I was involved with the purchase of a building that was built on two separate parcels; one fee simple and the other on a ground lease. The ground lease had about 20 heirs who owned an interest in it; some who hadn't spoken with each other for over 25 years, because of bad relationships within the family. Their attorney assured me that he would get everyone's signature necessary to the transaction. As I checked in with him regularly, he would tell me he was making progress, but was not always forthcoming with who he still needed to get signed up. The bottom line is that we were barely able to get it all signed up in time to close the transaction, due to the amount of time it took to get everyone's signature. Be sure to build in enough time or the ability to extend the time needed to get the necessary paperwork concluded required for the transaction.

Operating Budget

Most property management firms will have prepared an operating budget for the current year, and later in the calendar year, next year's operating budget. This budget will factor in any upcoming maintenance and needed repairs to the property. Always ask for the current year's operating budget and, if they have it, next year's budget as well. This will alert you to any expenditures planned for repairs, replacements, maintenance issues, code compliance issues, upgrades, refurbishment plans, and tenant improvement projects coming up. Some property managers are reluctant to hand it over and may give some excuse for not being able to. Don't just passively accept it. Insist you need to see it. If they say they can't, ask if there is anything that the ownership is trying to hide from you. Tell them it is important for you to review it. There is much to be learned and it will tell you a lot about what's happening with the building.

Property Tax Appeals

In most states, the property taxation process allows for an appeal if the property owner believes the tax assessment to be excessive or unfair. Since property taxes are such a large part of the operating expenses, it makes perfect sense to challenge the tax assessor's property tax bill so that you know you are getting the lowest possible assessment allowed. This can be done primarily through third party tax consultants who specialize in doing just that, property tax appeals. They have the local expertise in property values and processes in getting your tax bill reduced. This is generally done on a percentage of the savings or negotiated fee basis. All in all, it's a worthwhile fee paid to save a good chunk of money. It's too important to overlook, although some property owners do.

Important Note: Prior to removing contingencies, make sure that all property tax appeals have been processed. If tax appeals have not been processed, you need to make sure that the new tax amount is reflected in the underwriting and in line with what was disclosed in the offering memorandum, if the property is being marketed. If there are any special assessments to the property you need to get copies of them and make sure they were disclosed as part of the offering memorandum or any documentation provided by seller.

Depending upon the state, property taxes are assessed every one to three years. Make sure, if it's longer than one year, where you are in the cycle to determine when property tax increases will affect you. Also, get the contact information for any tax consultants that have been retained to ensure all tax appeals are submitted or in process.

CHAPTER 8

Underwriting and Financial Analysis

One of the most crucial processes of purchasing investment property is the financial analysis and underwriting. This process will not only determine what the property value is currently, but also, how much debt you can put on it and give you an idea of what value you can achieve upon execution of your exit strategy. In addition, you'll be able to determine where some savings can be gained in the operating expenses and any increases in the rental rate structure of the leases, both of which affects the bottom line and adds value to the property.

The following is a list of questions you need to answer as you're creating and underwriting the financial analysis of the property:

- What is the current in-place net operating income (NOI)? What does the NOI trend look like? Look over the trailing 12 months and forward 12 months to see if it drops, and if so, ask why this is happening. Perhaps a major tenant is downsizing or vacating.
- What is the expected sale price?
- What is the current occupancy? What is the historical occupancy for the past three years? Is it dropping? If so, you need to determine if this is a market that is continuing to lose tenancies or determine what some of the other possible problems you may uncover.
- How does the average rental rate in the building compare with its competitive set (the other properties the subject property competes with)? Are they above market or

below market? What are the rental rates of the most recent leases done in the building? Are they above or below market?

- What is the rollover for the current rent roll? Is the rollover (upcoming tenant lease expirations) stated rent above or below market?

- Are there any termination options in the current leases? (You need to constantly update your financial analysis as you get feedback during your initial investigation, due diligence and tenant interviews).

- How are the expenses running compared to other buildings in the area? Are they higher? If so, what categories and why? Are the expenses lower? If so, are there deferred capital expenditures and maintenance? What are the expense trends for the past three years? Make sure you come to a conclusion as to why a particular category is higher or lower for that matter.

- Are the pass-through of operating expenses going to continue or drop if expenses are lowered? If so, an adjustment should be determined that will more accurately reflect the change in future income.

- What is the condition of the tenant improvements in the rollover space coming up as well as the vacant suites? Are they typically built out and need only minor improvements and modifications or are they built out for a specific use and most likely will require a "gut and re-do" on the entire space? A realistic budget for tenant improvements should be assigned to each suite/unit or apartment, if necessary, in order to come up with a good monetary number for tenant improvements required.

- What is the market leasing commission being paid for new leases and renewals? What is the average tenant improvement allowance in the market for new and renewal leases?

- What are the current lease comparables for the competitive buildings in the area?
- What kinds of rental concessions, if any, are being offered?
- Are there broker incentives being offered by the competition? What are they and for which buildings?
- Are there common area upgrades that are needed? If so, you need to budget for them and place them in your underwriting.
- What kinds of conditions are the building systems in, i.e., roof; mechanical and electrical systems; elevators need modernizing? Do they need replacing, repairing or upgrading? Make sure you're plugging in replacement or repair dollars, or reserves for them.
- Does the building need to be brought up to current code compliance for: ADA; elevators; fire sprinklers; fire/life safety; OSHA compliant window cleaning roof supports, etc.? You need to contact the local municipal building and safety department authority to make sure there are no existing code violations or pending requirements that need to be made.
- Are there any environmental issues affecting the property? If so, you need to determine the cost or if you even want to move forward with the acquisition?
- Is the debt coverage ratio acceptable for your respective lender(s)? What is the highest loan to value that the lender will provide? Is the NOI at least 25-30% higher than the debt service? Check with the lender to make sure the numbers work in compliance with their requirements or you can be wasting time on a deal that is not doable.
- Do the operating expenses in the offering memorandum, if any, reflect the same expenses found in the reports provided by the seller? If not, where are the discrepancies? There may be reason to go back and ask

for a price reduction if the expenses were understated in the offering.

- Are there any association fees or dues required to be paid by the building's ownership?
- Are there any services required by an existing tenant in the building such as security or parking attendants?
- Are there any additional HVAC hours required in any leases and provided at the building owner's expense to any of the existing tenants?
- Will the lender require any holdbacks of funds or reserves for upcoming building improvements or re-leasing and/or lease renewals? If so, how much?
- How will the parking income be affected upon expiration or termination of leases?
- Is your exit strategy reflecting a realistic cap rate upon the sale of the property? (Usually estimated to be at least one point higher than the going in cap, as a general rule.)
- Are there adequate reserves plugged into your underwriting to cover any immediate repairs and future replacement of necessary items such as cooling towers; chillers; roof, etc.?
- Are there any amenities that could be added to the building such as a common conference room; a work out facility; bike racks; smoking and/or seating areas, etc., which would enhance the lease ability of the building? If so, what would be the cost? Is it justifiable?

This list is not complete or exhaustive; however, it gives you enough information gathering to cover a lot of ground in your underwriting process. Each property is unique in some way, as well as each geographic location. There are some locales that have expenses to the property that are unique to that particular region, i.e. snow and ice removal; sinkhole problems; seismic concerns and retrofits on equipment, just to name a few.

You need to continually be on guard as to what information is being given to you and its validity, because the end result is once you own the property, it's your problem to deal with.

Make sure you're verifying information and are comfortable with your findings. Assume Nothing. Underwriting is an ongoing process during your due diligence and beyond, until closing. Even then, you'll be looking back to see how accurate your analysis was during the time you own the property.

CHAPTER 9

Additional Items to Explore for Industrial, Retail, and Multi-Family Properties

Each property type has its unique qualities and issues that should be investigated or addressed. For the most part, the information contained in this handbook for conducting due diligence on commercial properties is relative and applicable across all the genres: office; industrial; retail or multi-family residential.

Obviously, the questions asked need to be tailored to the specific type of property that is being purchased.

The following information can be considered for each of the property types. It is in no way intended to be conclusive nor exhaustive. It is offered for additional information gathering purposes in the event you are not entirely familiar with the specific issues and items for the respective property type.

Industrial
- Capacity of utilities, i.e. electrical; water; gas
- Minimum/maximum floor loads/thicknesses
- Confirmation of interior clear heights beneath the sprinkler and structural components
- Adequate ingress/egress from the site
- Loading/unloading doors/dock high or ground level
- Potential issues with current neighbors
- Zoning classification
- Municipal restrictions
- Local and state political climate

- Ground water contamination present or close proximity to the site
- Site erosion and drainage adequacy/compliance
- Adequate maneuvering clearance for trucks on the site
- Asphalt and concrete condition
- Adequate water pressure and coverage for most users
- Dock levelers
- Dock cushions or shelters
- Safety locks and lights
- Trailer lights
- Truck well drainage
- Column spacing for equipment layout and warehouse racking

The purchaser of industrial properties should consider not only the physical aspects of the building and property, but also consider what could possibly have a negative impact for future users and/or purchaser from a business operations standpoint. You want to be able to identify any potential problems before you own the property.

It would be a good idea to get the opinion of some local brokers who specialize in industrial properties to give you an unbiased opinion as to what they believe to be the positive and negative aspects of the property. The listing broker will not generally be the one to point out any negative issues regarding the property.

Retail

- Demographics for the site location
- Ease of ingress/egress
- Street exposure
- Signage visibility and restrictions
- Adequate parking available?
- Are there any tenants such as a nail, fitness facility, beauty salon or other parking intensive use which will negatively impact the customer parking?

- Where do the tenants/employees park?
- Bay depths
- Window mullion spacing
- Maximum ceiling heights
- HVAC package units—size, age, condition and tonnage
- Tenant mix
- Common area maintenance expenses
- Any restrictions of tenants for the location?
- Exclusivity provisions in the leases?
- Any percentage rent provisions in any of the leases?
- Do any of the tenants have multiple locations nearby?
- Historical occupancy
- Turnover rate if it is a retail center
- Financial viability of the tenants
- Municipal code violations pending
- Any current tenants who have a detrimental use to the center?
- Is there a tenant association and common marketing fund?

Retail properties require an in depth due diligence that is specialized and must be adequately explored so that the investor is relatively comfortable with the tenant mix (if in a retail shopping center or strip center); the demographics of the area where it's located; and the various nuances that come with owning retail properties.

Retail property is going through a metamorphosis of sorts. Mainly, because of people's shopping habits that have been altered by Amazon and other online providers of commerce.

That doesn't mean that every property will be affected. What it does mean is that if you're an investor, you need to consider the type of retail property it is you own or are looking to invest in, and how it may be affected in the future, if you were to have to repurpose it. For example, let's say you own a larger retail property such as a grocery store that is approximately 25,000-30,000 square feet. The footprint for many grocery store chains have expanded to 40,000-50,000 square feet. If the current tenant moves out, what other type of tenants would be interested in that size building in the market and location it's in. Is it divisible and if so, how will it lay out? Will the bay depths be too deep, say 50 feet plus, making it undesirable because of the "bowling alley" affect?

Perhaps you own a 3000-5000 square foot retail building on a major street with other retailers in the area. It may make sense to divide it in two or three spaces, then rent it out, thereby diversifying your risk, or even increasing the income.

It pays to consult with the seasoned retail commercial brokers in the area you are considering investing in. They can educate you on the property/center; the property's competitive set; the general perception of the property and retail area in which it's located and what it will take to keep it leased. They can provide you with a wealth of information about your prospective investment.

Multi-Family Residential

The multi-family residential arena is the most popular of the commercial real estate genres.

Mainly because it's the most easily understood and prevalent. After all, everyone needs a place to live. It too requires its own set of specialized nuances investigated when conducting due diligence during the potential purchase.

- General vacancy of similar age, condition properties in the area
- Tenant mix, i.e. single/studio, one, two and three bedroom units
- Overall condition of the property
- Rent controlled?
- Eviction rules, timing, procedure
- In-place rents vs. market rents
- Operating expenses compared to competitive properties
- Length of leases / month-to-month?
- Parking and guest parking adequate?

- Any street parking restrictions?
- Crime statistics in the neighborhood
- Security issues on the property or surrounding properties
- Age and condition of cars parked in the garage or parking areas (Best to check this out in the evening when most people are at home. This will give you an idea of the socioeconomic mix of the tenants.)
- Retail amenities in the area
- Municipal parks in the area and their proximity to the property
- Schools and distance to them from the property
- Access to public transportation
- Access to highways, main roads and freeways
- Laundry facilities on site
- Other amenities such as club room; work out facility with equipment
- Pets allowed (one indication of some buildings high turnover rate is their willingness to allow pets)
- Utilities and/or cable TV included?
- Concessions being offered (i.e. free rent? This is a sign of a soft rental market.)
- Major employers in the area (Any news of recent or potential future layoffs?)

These are some of the issues worth exploring when considering and involved with the purchase of multi-family residential properties. You may want to look at the units available for rent in the competitive properties of the one you're looking to purchase to get a better idea of what the competition is offering.

By taking the time to thoroughly explore the issues, questions and relevant items with other professionals, such as property management companies, commercial brokers specializing in multi-family residential, you will be further enlightened. They will be able to help you fill in the blanks and guide you to making an informed and intelligent decision before you own the property.

The time spent in conducting proper and thorough due diligence will pay you many times over and way out of proportion to your time invested. Too many investors do not give this important aspect of investing in commercial real estate its rightful priority. This is mainly because they haven't learned the proper procedure and system to do it correctly.

CHAPTER 10

Heading Towards the Finish Line

You've completed much of your physical due diligence and record review (however, this is continuously updated through the entire process) and are ready to work on the lender required documents, such as estoppel certificates, subordination and non-disturbance agreements, as well as the final appraisal for the loan.

Be certain you haven't missed anything by going through your email chains to see if there were items and answers that were promised but not delivered; things that could have slipped through the cracks. If you wait until the last minute, things will get hectic and you will most likely forget about them. It's a horrible feeling to find out that you never received something that you were waiting for and now that the transaction is finalized, you own the property, and have no idea where to find it. Even worse, it now is going to cost you a lot of money because you don't have it. It's a hard lesson to learn that way.

Now is the time to go back through your emails, notes, memos, and discussions with your team members, to make sure nothing is being forgotten or left out. **Review your Due Diligence Document Checklist (included at the back of the book and on my website at www.impactcoachingsystems.com/courses, under the Resources tab) to see if you received everything you asked for.** This is time well spent. If you slow down and methodically go through your due diligence materials and questions, you will find that there are usually some things that may have been overlooked or not thoroughly checked out or yet received.

Once your due diligence contingency period is up and your earnest money deposit is "hard" i.e. nonrefundable, much of the negotiating leverage you have has been spent. That's why you need to be certain ALL the answers you were looking for are satisfactory and no loose ends remain. Generally, most of the negotiations are going to happen just prior to your expiration of the due diligence period.

If in fact, you are going to ask the seller for a price reduction or a contribution towards the repair or replacement of equipment, or some other item or issue, you need to be able to justify your request. First and foremost, it should be a legitimate reason and not some fabricated excuse to ask for a discount. That will only serve to alienate the seller and tarnish your reputation as a buyer in the commercial real estate market. You definitely do not want that to happen. It's a very tight community and word travels fast. Remember that people buy people first, no matter what the industry.

One way to make your request, is to write the seller an email stating the facts of your findings, including some bids for the replacement or repair, and why you believe it would be fair and equitable for them to provide the credit. You can then state that once you have an agreement with them that you are prepared to remove your contingencies and move forward in finalizing the transaction, if you are ready to do so. You must be prepared to remove all your contingencies before proposing the discount or credit. Otherwise, the seller will not feel there's any benefit to conceding to it. If they see you're ready to move forward and commit by letting your earnest money deposit become non-refundable, they are more likely to agree or try to negotiate with you.

There is no guarantee that they will give you what you are asking for. If not, you can try to negotiate a settlement with them or make the decision to walk from the deal. I'm a big believer in always having a walk away position. If you do not, then the seller will know and remain inflexible in their position. I've canceled escrow on some deals and had the seller come back to work things out. In others, they never came back and we walked away from the deal.

Here's my suggestion and a strategy that I've found to be helpful: Have an ideal, best case scenario, which is close to your first offer price: "I'd really like to buy it at this price." Then a target price range: "I would still buy it if were in this price range." And finally: "I will walk away from the deal if it is above this price." That way you have a strategy in mind beforehand to work with and you know ahead of time what your position is, so you feel more confident while negotiating. It also helps to remove a lot of the emotion from the process. This has served me well over the years. It's easy to get emotionally involved in the process if you feel you must own the property. It's best to take as much of that emotion out of the equation.

Estoppel Certificates

Estoppel certificates are the statements executed by the tenants that are the verification of the key terms of the lease and that neither tenant nor landlord is in default. Tenants will note any discrepancies or outstanding issues with the current landlord.

Before sending estoppel certificates out to the tenants, be sure the form has been approved by the lender.

Make sure that you review the prepared estoppels before they are sent out to the tenants, and then review them when they are sent back by the tenants for verification.

Don't send any estoppels received by tenants with discrepancies or issues that affect the lease terms to the lender before receiving an explanation of the issue or discrepancy.

The required estoppels should be delivered by the lender.

SNDAs (Subordination & Non-Disturbance Agreements)

This form is required by the lender and should be delivered to the required tenants at the same time as the estoppels. This form is sometimes dealt with post-closing.

Lender Required Property Appraisal

Most lenders require a property appraisal on the property, which most likely the loan amount is subject to, and which is paid for by the buyer. You can't take for granted that everything is going to work out fine with it and not pay attention to what the appraiser is going to come up with as a final value for the property.

You need to monitor and talk to the appraiser to make sure: he has the proper information such as the most up to date rent roll; pending transactions, if any, and if helpful, the most recent lease and sale comparables, that help justify the purchase price being paid; the expenses that you will be running the property at, i.e. showing cost cutting; any additional income that the property is generating should be provided, such as roof/cell site income; storage space income; parking income; and make sure that they are accounting for any rental increases; pass through of operating expenses and anything else that will enhance the value of the property that you can provide them.

Although many of the appraisers do not wish to speak with the borrower, it is necessary to make that initial contact with them to make sure that you're not going to get "short-changed" on the appraisal, because they weren't provided all they could have been to increase the value of the appraisal.

It can't be stressed enough; if you're not being proactive with the appraiser and let the appraisal process go on "auto-pilot", you run a high chance of getting a lower appraisal and therefore a less desirable loan amount and potentially higher holdback amounts. I'm a big believer you need to become more like a "fighter-pilot" and become armed and ready with all the information you can provide the appraiser, to help them bolster the appraised value, so that you reduce the risk of them coming in with a lower amount on the appraisal. It's very difficult to "back-pedal" with the lender once they get the appraisal and try to convince them the property is worth more. Better to circumvent that problem by being prepared and providing the necessary "ammunition" to help the appraiser get to a higher value.

Get your mortgage broker involved as well in helping to work with the appraiser. Also, ask your broker or the listing broker to provide sale and lease comparables that help justify the purchase price of the property that you can provide to the appraiser. I have not come across an appraiser in over 30 years of working in the commercial real estate industry, that refused to accept the sale and lease comparables offered to them. Why would they? Your helping them make their job that much easier. It's always better to have someone other than yourself, who is not at the same firm, giving their input as well.

I recently came across a scenario that helps illustrate how this can work. We were asked to help a client to find a small industrial building of about 5000 square feet, in a very tight submarket where there was little product available. A building came up, that they found, that was listed. They sent us the information and we called the listing broker. We were told it just fell out of escrow and it was available. The listing price was very high. It had been owned by the same person for over 40 years and they had recently passed away. The heirs were disposing of the property. It was also being touted as a "work-live" property, since the owner had a residential unit as part of it and had resided there. There were "work-live" lofts located next to it that had been recently developed, so the listing broker assumed that this property was also zoned for it as well. Whence, the big asking price. It turned out, after we checked with the city zoning department, that is was not.

We informed the prospective purchasers that it was over-priced for the area. They insisted that the building was perfect for their needs and they didn't mind over-paying since they planned on being there many years and believed in what was happening in the area with all the new improvements and amenities.

We spoke to their lender and asked that we get the appraiser's contact info so we could meet them out at the property. We also found out from the lender that the building had been in escrow three other times, but didn't appraise. We suspected that may be the case after speaking with the broker.

We did meet the appraiser at the property, with a large note-book stuffed with sale and lease comparables in a 10-15-mile radius, due to a lack of available comparable information in the immediate surrounding area. We also supplemented it with in-formation, talking up the all the recent developments and future developments in the works, that helped to improve the values of the surrounding area of the subject building. We went through all the information we put together there at the property when we met them, so we could discuss our findings in more detail. We then followed up with them to make sure they had every-thing they needed to help get to the value we were looking to achieve. They confirmed that they had everything they needed and were comfortable with the value of the property. The lender got the appraised value they needed to make the loan and ev-eryone was happy when it closed escrow. It's doubtful it would have been appraised at the needed value, without having been proactive with the appraiser.

Closing Statement

One of the most important items in due diligence is to prop-erly review the closing statement prepared by escrow before fi-nalizing the transaction. If you're not careful in scrutinizing it, it can cost you dearly. Remember always, the seller wants to get as much as possible upon the sale of the property, even if that means loading up additional items as a credit to them on the closing statement. This can take the form of many different items, such as: tenant improvements; leasing commissions; capi-tal improvements; prorations of fees and licenses paid; inspec-tions; service contracts; supplies; personal property; prorations of property taxes; annual membership or association fees, just to name a few.

In addition to the seller's credits, you need to watch for lender and escrow fees. These can sometimes get added into the closing statement without noticing how they are being assessed to the buyer, i.e. inspection fees; legal fees; additional documentation fees, e.g., lease review fees, which should be questioned, but try hard to eliminate, or at the very least negotiate down. There are some buyer/sellers who are extremely proficient at loading additional expenses to pass on to the other party.

If you're not paying close attention, it could cost you a tremendous sum of money.

Make sure prorations of operating expenses are properly prorated under each line item and get back up information on each amount, i.e. copies of checks; paid invoices; lien releases, in the case of tenant improvement work or capital work completed, etc.

In prorating fees on service contracts or annual inspections, be sure you're only prorating the amounts allocated for the closing month. Do not credit the seller for annual inspections, as they are purchased as part of the asset.

Any credits or charges allocated to the seller must be verified. Make sure there are only those credits and/or charges that were agreed to in the purchase and sale agreement. This cannot be over emphasized. Once the transaction is completed, it is very difficult to get reimbursed. It is worth the extra time and effort spent in carefully scrutinizing the closing statement expenses and allocations.

Important note: Always be sure that you tell the escrow officer that no closing statement is released to seller or lender until it is cleared and they get approval by you. In addition, the buyer's closing statement, when purchasing a property, shows only the buyer's side of the transaction and not combined.

Have the escrow officer include all buyer costs, i.e. survey; third party reports; buyer expenses; insurance; commissions; etc. to be paid through escrow at the close. All deposits and fees paid, i.e. loan application fees; rate lock fees; etc. are included as buyer's credits. Also, make sure all lender fees, impound/reserve accounts are in line with the loan application terms. If you are assuming a loan, be sure that you are getting proper credit for reserves and impounds. This applies equally when you are the seller. Make sure you're getting credited properly for any reserves and impounds that were put aside by the lender. Have your mortgage broker read through and verify these as well.

It is always a good idea to have another set of eyes to go over the closing statement. Someone who knows what they're looking for. After looking at a number of versions, it's quite easy to overlook an item.

This is where most buyers are anxious to get the process over with. They are mentally and emotionally drained from going through all the various aspects of the transaction. Inspections, sifting through paperwork and records, reviewing financials, interviewing tenants, going through the loan application and appraisal process, chasing the seller down for information for answers and backup substantiation. It's no wonder that most buyers want it over with and just want to close the escrow.

That's why it's so important to slow down at this point and sift through all your emails with the various requests to the seller and their representatives. Also, speak with your team members, such as your attorney, inspectors, accountant, and anyone who was involved with helping you with your investigation and due diligence. Find out if they have any outstanding questions or concerns that haven't been addressed or answered properly. Remember, this is your last shot at getting all you can from the seller while they are still motivated to get the transaction closed.

By being patient and diligent about getting all your questions answered, getting back up substantiation where needed from the seller, and questioning the debits and expenses on the preliminary closing statement, it will pay off. Sometimes more than you would ever had realized, unless you went through this process slowly and carefully.

It's painful to discover after escrow has closed that you overlooked something that could have saved or made you a good chunk of money, had you spent the time necessary to scrutinize all the numbers methodically.

In Conclusion

Due Diligence, if performed properly and thoroughly, will prevent you from experiencing major setbacks and expenses, or keep you from making an investment that you should not. It should never be taken lightly or for granted. Every item should be scrutinized.

Assume Nothing. However, if you are to assume anything, assume there are a large amount of problems waiting to be discovered which could save you a ton of money and headaches, if you catch them; because the reality is there are always issues.

You are virtually throwing money away by not performing a thorough due diligence on property you're looking to purchase.

This handbook was written to give the novice a foundation to work from and to provide further enlightenment to the experienced investor on some important issues that they may not have thought about previously, as well as serve as a reminder/checklist. I still use it today as such. Many of my readers have told me they use it as a reference tool and keep it handy when conducting due diligence on a property. It's like a "pilot's checklist". There are too many things to remember. We need reminding as much as we need learning.

Whoever may be conducting it, due diligence is an ongoing learning experience and you want to constantly hone your skills. Constantly strive to be the best at it. If you do, it will pay off greatly and save you money, countless problems and headaches to deal with later. You will often find value enhancers that you would not normally be aware of because you have trained your eyes and ears to seek them out as you're performing your due diligence. **Visit my website at** www.impactcoachingsystems.com

for valuable forms and resources available there at no charge. Also, check out my Due Diligence Video Course at impactcoachingsystems.com/courses. **To receive a 20% discount off the video course use the code: DDHB20 at checkout.**

Remember, a successful due diligence leads to greater buyer peace of mind and less (or hopefully no) post-closing surprises. Done properly, it will also save you a ton of money and ensure the proper investment decision is made, to buy or not to buy.

Best of luck in your commercial real estate investing!

If you believe this information was helpful and could benefit others, I'd like to ask a big favor of you. Would you please leave a review of the book on Amazon.com? I would greatly appreciate it. Thank you!

Sample Lease Abstract Form

Property Address:
5950 Topanga Canyon Boulevard
Woodland Hills, CA 91367

Premises: Suite # _____
Commencement Date: January 1, 2002
Expiration Date: December 31, 2008
Rentable Area: _____ square feet
Tenant's Prorata Share: _____% – 194,887 total rentable area

Base Rent:
1/01/02 to 12/31/03 $
1/01/03 to 12/31/04 $
1/01/05 to 12/31/05 $
1/01/06 to 12/31/06 $
1/01/07 to 12/31/07 $
1/01/08 to 12/31/08 $

Lease Term: — 84 months
Gross Lease Amount: $ _____

Rental Abatement: First rental payment due _____
(Page 1)

Operating Expenses: Base Year 2003
(Landlord notice due by 4/01 each year)
(Page 3)
(Page 5)

Security Deposit: $ _____ (to be refunded at month 25)

(Page 18)
Guarantor(s): None
Landlords: BH Enterprises, L.P.
Notice Address: Attn: Regional Manager
　　　　　　　　　4929 25th Avenue
　　　　　　　　　Denver, CO 80237
Tenants: _____
Notice Address: Attn:_____
　　　　　　　　　5950 Topanga Canyon Boulevard # _____
　　　　　　　　　Woodland Hills, CA 91367
Copy to:
NGR Advisors
Attn: Brian Hennessey
5950 Topanga Canyon Boulevard, # _____
Woodland Hills, CA 91367

Lease Payments:
BH Realty Investors, L.P.
4929 25th Avenue
Denver, CO 80237

Exhibits:
　A.) Premises
　B.) Rules
　C.) Work Letter (Turnkey – @$30/SF)
　D.) Parking (4.0/1000)
　E.) Right of First Refusal (30-Day Response)
　F.) Extension Option (Notice Due 3/08 – 9/08)

Subletting (Page 13): Tenant request deemed to be approved 30 days after Landlord receives subtenant financial statement and sublease terms & conditions.

Landlord and Tenant to divide any "net" profits 50/50. $500 toward Landlord's legal fees. S/L conditions do not apply if Tenant maintains 51% ownership in new entity.
Holding Over (Page 23): 150% after first 90 days of Hold Over.

(Exhibit E) Right of First Refusal: Landlord to give Tenant 30 days to accept lease terms & conditions offered by third party on adjacent space of 6,000 square feet. Term to run concurrent with existing lease. Improvements to be amortized over balance of lease terms.

Extension Option (Exhibit F): Tenant shall have a right to extend the lease with notice to Landlord between 3/08—9/08. Lease terms to be at 90% of market with improvements and brokerage fees amortized.

Miscellaneous Provisions:
   A.) Default/Landlord Remedies (Page 17)
   B.) Alterations (Page 10)
   C.) Notices (Page 30)

Due Diligence Checklist

Property Information
___ Updated/Existing ALTA Survey/Site Plan
___ Legal Description
___ Environmental Report (Phase I/II)
___ Property Condition Report
___ ADA Report
  Mechanical/Engineering Reports

Structural Report/Roof Report
___ Infrared Survey
___ Preliminary Title Report
___ Floor Plans (indicating: tenant location and square footage)
___ Space Measurement Studies (CAD drawing & detail of gross, usable and rentable sq. ft.)
___ Property Warranties (roof, mechanical, etc.)
___ Status of Deferred Maintenance Issues
___ Status on All Ongoing Capital Improvement (Construction Contract)
___ Vendor Service Contracts/Summary (including: union contract)
___ Description of Security/Life Safety Systems
___ Certificate of Occupancy/Building Permits (Fire Panel, Elevator, etc.)
___ Detailed Parking Schedule
___ List of All Code Violation
___ Association Documents
___ Land Lease

Tenant Information

___ Detailed Rent Roll Showing Rental Increases and All Other Charges

___ Leases, Amendments, Commencement Letters, Letter Agreements, Lease Abstracts, Sub-Leases, etc.

___ Standard Lease Form

___ Pending Leases and Correspondence

___ Landlord/Tenant Correspondence

___ Tenant Financials

___ Tenant Insurance Certificates

___ Schedule of Historical Tenant Improvement Costs and Concessions

___ Historical Occupancy Report

___ List of All Tenants with Outstanding TI's & LC's indicating owner/tenant obligations

___ List of Tenants with Scheduled Rent Concessions

Financial Information

___ Detailed Operating Statements (2005, 2006, YTD 2007)

___ 2007 Detailed Operating Budget

___ Detailed CAM Reconciliation/Expense Recovery Worksheets (2005, 2006 and all

___ existing base year)

___ List of Current Operating Expense Billing Details and Monthly Tenant Invoices

___ Real Estate Tax Bill (two year)

___ Real Estate Tax Appeals

___ Historical and Budgeted Capital Expenditures/Tenant Improvement

___ Loan Documents – Notes, Loan Agreements, Current Balance/ Payment Info

___ Utility Bills for last 24 month

___ Utilities Contract

___ Recent A/R Report

___ Prior Month Tenant Statement

___ General Ledger for 2006 and YTD 2007

___ Security Deposit Ledger and List of Letters of Credit

___ Detail of All Allocated Salaries (including all accrued vacation and sick pay)

General Information

___ Personal Property Inventory List

___ Tool Inventory List

___ Litigation Pending or in Progress

___ List of Insurance Claims in the Last 5 Years

___ Broker Leasing and Commission Agreement

___ City Development Agreement

___ Property Management Agreement

EXHIBIT C

Due Diligence Document Checklist

Property Information

___ Updated/Existing ALTA Survey/Site Plan

___ Recent Environmental Report (Phase I/II)

___ Recent Property Condition Report

___ Recent ADA Report

___ Recent Mechanical/Engineering Reports

___ Recent Structural Report/Roof Report

___ Recent Infrared Survey

___ Preliminary Title Report

___ Floor Plans (indicating: tenant location and square footage)

___ Space Measurement Studies (CAD drawings & detail of gross, usable and rentable sq. ft.)

___ Property Warranties (roof, mechanical, etc.)

___ Status of Deferred Maintenance Issues

___ Status on All Ongoing Capital Improvements

___ Vendor Service Contracts/Summary (including: union contract)

___ Description of Security/Life Safety Systems

___ Certificates of Occupancy/Building Permits (Fire Panel, Elevator, etc.)

___ Detailed Parking Schedule

___ List of All Code Violations

___ Association Documents

___ Land Lease

Tenant Information

___ Detailed Rent Roll Showing Rental Increases and All Other Charges

___ Leases, Amendments, Commencement Letters, Letter Agreements, Lease Abstracts, Sub-Leases, etc.

___ Landlord/Tenant Correspondence

___ Tenant Financials

___ Schedule of Historical Tenant Improvement Costs and Concessions

___ Historical Occupancy Report

___ List of All Tenants with Outstanding TI's & LC's

Financial Information

___ Detailed Operating Statements (Past three years & YTD)

___ Current Year Detailed Operating Budget

___ Detailed CAM Reconciliation/Expense Recovery Worksheets (Past Two Years)

___ List of Current Operating Expense Billing Details and Monthly Tenant Invoices

___ Real Estate Tax Bills (two years)

___ Real Estate Tax Appeals

___ Historical and Budgeted Capital Expenditures/Tenant Improvements

___ Loan Documents – Notes, Loan Agreements, Current Balance/ Payment Info

___ Utility Bills for last 24 months

___ Recent A/R Report

___ General Ledger for last 12 months

___ Security Deposit Ledger and List of Letters of Credit

___ Detail of All Allocated Salaries (including all accrued vacation and sick pay)

General Information

___ Personal Property Inventory List

___ Tool Inventory List

___ Litigation Pending or in Progress

___ List of Insurance Claims in the Last 3 Years

Sample Tenant Questionnaire Letter

Date: _____
Tenant: _____
Suite: _____

Dear _____ (Tenant),

As you may know, we are in the process of potentially acquiring the building and would appreciate your cooperation in answering the following questions, so that we can complete our due diligence analysis for this property:

1. How long have you been working in the building?
2. Why did your company select this building versus other buildings?
3. Has the landlord been generally responsive in meeting your needs?
4. Do you currently have any disputes with the landlord?
5. Do you have any outstanding service request?
6. What is the most common service request you make to the landlord?
7. Is your suite generally too hot, too cold or comfortable most of the time?
8. Are there any water leaks? Have there been any water leaks?
9. Have there been any unusual odors?
10. Have there been any power outages?
11. Are the hallways generally kept clean and neat?
12. Are the bathrooms kept clean?
13. Does the janitorial service adequately clean your suite?

14. Is the exterior of the building kept clean and neat?
15. Do you feel safe walking to your car in the evening?
16. What do you like about the location of your offices? What do you dislike?
17. Can you always find a parking space?
18. What additional amenities or services would you like added to the building?
19. What improvements would you like added to your suite?
20. Is your suite "crowded?" Do you need more or less space?
21. Is your current business expanding, contracting or staying about the same?
22. If your lease came up for renewal now, would you consider staying in the building?
23. Do you anticipate remaining in the building once your lease expires?
24. Any problems with the elevator?
25. Any problems with HVAC?
26. Any problems with the plumbing?

We would like to thank you for your cooperation. If you have any suggestions or requests to make your offices more comfortable and productive, please let us know.

Sincerely,

Acknowledgments

First and foremost, I thank God for all the many blessings I am aware of and unaware of that I have in my life. He is the Giver of ALL gifts. You will see His hand working in ALL aspects of your life, if you will just look for it. When you do, and express gratitude each time you notice, you will see your life taking on a whole new meaning. It will open the way for more to come to you in all areas of your life. How do I know? I've proven it to myself. And you can too.

There are many people that I could thank for all the lessons I learned throughout my commercial real estate career, but there are just too many to mention, and I wouldn't want to forget someone. So, for all those folks who helped me learn the ropes, I am grateful and express my sincere appreciation.

I'd like to express my gratitude to Todd Gallapo, Kimberley Anderson, Jen Montgomery and Vanessa Goodman at Meat and Potatoes Design Studio for their many talents and skills at designing the book cover. They are super-talented and super-nice folks.

I'd like also to thank Bud Smith for his contribution to this third revision of the book. His input and contribution to the Mechanical and Physical Inspections chapter are invaluable. Bud's extensive 40+ years of experience has taught me and many others a vast amount of information on the physical and mechanical aspects of commercial properties. He teaches energy conservation methods and engineering principles to asset managers, property managers and corporate level engineers. He's been a leader and innovator in his field for many years.

Resources

Websites

AIR Lease Forms Manual

These manuals provide a step-by-step guide to understanding and using the AIR's commercial real estate contract forms. Both volumes are written by the experts who create, review, update, and provide training for all the AIR Forms. Visit their website at: www.airformsmanual.com. You can find out how to get the forms at: http://www.airea.com.

LoopNet.com

LoopNet.com is the most heavily trafficked commercial real estate website, with over 5 million average monthly unique visitors according to Google Analytics*. Their registered members generate over 60 million page views per month. Find and list properties for sale and lease in your marketplace.

CoStar.com

The CoStar Group brands combine research, technology, innovative tools, and powerful marketing to connect the world's leading commercial real estate professionals with the data, insights and property owners. It is subscription based and is widely accepted as the industry standard for most commercial brokerage firms, as well as multiple listing services. By the way, CoStar owns LoopNet.

Cityfeet.com
Listings of various commercial properties for lease mainly in major metropolitan areas.

Google Earth
A "must have" for anyone who is looking at properties for investment. Why drive there first, when you can take a first look with a birds-eye view of the property? Download it and have the icon on your desktop for easy access.

Multifamilyinsiders.com
This site is all about apartments including: management; trends; investment; leasing, etc. Excellent web source.

Spaceforlease.com
A commercial real estate listing site for leasing opportunities only.

CREedge.com
It's the top website to find commercial real estate professionals, along with a lot of other great content being added regularly for commercial real estate resources.

Books
- *You Can Negotiate Anything* by Herb Cohen
- *Getting More: How You Can Negotiate to Succeed in Work and Life* by Stuart Diamond
- *Secrets of Power Negotiating* by Roger Dawson
- *Getting to Yes* by Roger Fisher & William Ury
- *Influence: The Psychology of Persuasion* by Robert Cialdini
- *Confessions of a Real Estate Entrepreneur* by James A. Randel
- *The Complete Guide to Buying and Selling Apartment Buildings* by Steve Berges

Software

Argussoftware.com

ARGUS products have become the industry standard and provide the complete solution for transacting, managing and growing your commercial real estate portfolio. The industry's leading owners, managers, financial institutions, REITs, brokerages and appraisers trust ARGUS solutions to improve the visibility and flow of information throughout their critical business processes. These processes include asset management, asset valuation, portfolio management, budgeting, forecasting, financial reporting, acquisitions and dispositions, and underwriting. This software is fairly sophisticated and requires comprehensive training. Financial institutions will generally want to see an Argus financial run on bigger properties so they can manipulate the assumptions within the financial analysis to comply with their underwriting guidelines to see if the property meets their requirements. For the average commercial real estate investor, this software is more than is needed or necessary.

Realdata.com

Comparative Lease Analysis Software. Analyze commercial and industrial real estate leases easily and accurately using RealData's Comparative Lease Analysis software. Just enter the terms and conditions in this fill-in-the-blanks program and in minutes you can compare the true cost or benefit of up to six scenarios.

Procalc.com

The industry standard lease analysis software program, currently used by thousands of commercial real estate professionals allowing users to analyze and compare leases from the tenant, landlord, sub-lessor's or purchaser's perspective. If you are involved in the negotiation of leasing or purchasing commercial, office, industrial or retail space you need ProCalc. Excellent program for owners/landlords, brokers, property and asset managers. Customer service second to none.

Institutional Real Estate, Inc.

IREI publishes a diversified portfolio of news magazines, special reports and directories for the benefit of global institutional real estate investment community. Each publication provides subscribers with news, insights and perspective on the trends and events shaping the investment landscape in private equity real estate. Highly recommended. Visit their website at: www. irei.com

Financial Analyst / Argus Software Specialist

Wayne Edmondson

Wayne.edmondson@gmail.com; 714.734.0162

Cost Segregation

Greg K. Bryant, CCSP Managing Partner Bedford

17 Commerce Drive, Suite 7

Bedford, NH 03110; 603.641.2600 x302

www.bedfordteam.com

Sample Forms

Sample drafts of these and other useful forms are available for review and downloading at www.impactcoachingsystems.com.

- Competitive Set Building Comparable Sheet
- Competitive Set Lease Comparable Sheet
- Sample Proposals and Request for Proposal (Available Online)
- Sample *AIR Standard Multi-Tenant Office Lease – Gross (Available Online)
- Sample *AIR Standard Multi-Tenant Office Lease – Net (Available Online)
- Sample *AIR Rules and Regulations for Standard Office Lease (Available Online)
- Sample *AIR Standard Industrial/Commercial Multi-Tenant Lease – Net
- Sample *AIR Standard Industrial/Commercial Single-Tenant Lease – Net

- Sample *AIR Standard Multi-Tenant Shopping Center Lease – Net
- Sample Credit Report Authorization
- Sample Tenant Application

Notice: No part of any of the AIR Commercial Real Estate Forms may be reproduced in any form without written permission from the AIR Commercial Real Estate Association.

Glossary of Real Estate Terms

Available at www.impactcoachingsystems.com under RESOURCES.

Consultation Services

Brian offers his consulting services on creating value, cash flow, and navigating the due diligence process for individuals as well as groups. He will teach you the necessary skills to gain a greater understanding and execution of conducting a thorough investigation of commercial real estate investments for acquisition. Once these strategies and principles have been learned and incorporated into your skillset you will have them for life to reduce your risk, or your client's risk, of making a bad investment and help to create greater value.

Here are a few of the ways his consulting services can be structured:

1. **One-on-one instruction.** He will work with you one-on-one to teach you the step-by-step instructions in detail about how to conduct a thorough and proper due diligence investigation. You can custom design a program with him to correlate with your specific interests or choose a pre-designed general program that he provides his consulting clients.

2. **Have Brian Conduct Due Diligence on a Property.** Hire Brian to conduct the actual due diligence process and teach you or your team as he goes through it so you can learn as he goes through the transaction with you.

3. **Team Instruction.** Have you and your team learn all the important details and instruction to incorporate into your acquisition process. This will allow for the entire team to know all the necessary steps for each team member and their respective roles when conducting due diligence. Once your team has these skills in their tool set they will

perform like a well-oiled machine and will be less likely to miss important items and issues and let things fall through the cracks.

4. **Specific Issues and Concerns Needed to be Addressed.** Hire Brian to discuss only specific issues and concerns you need help with, as needed.

5. **"Deep Dive" Consultation** – Spend the day with Brian. You can spend the day with Brian and ask him all the questions you'd like or learn all you can from him about a specific transaction, or any way you want to structure the visit.

Please contact Brian Hennessey to discuss rates and how you may be able to customize a program that best suits you and your needs. He can be reached at 818.371.0311 or brian@ impactcoachingsystems.com

About the Author

Brian Hennessey has been in the commercial real estate industry for over 30 years as: a commercial broker; a Senior Vice President of Acquisitions/Dispositions and also ran his own real estate syndication/ asset management company. He has represented a number of Fortune 500 Tenants including: Bank of America, The Walt Disney Company and Bax-

ter Healthcare. With over 12 million square feet of sale and lease transactions; some of which were with some of the largest owner/ landlords in the country, a wealth of experience was accumulated.

"The Due Diligence Handbook for Commercial Real Estate" was written originally as a personal reference tool/checklist because of the many facets and volume of information that is needed to be remembered for each transaction.

He conducts seminars that teach the principles in the book in greater detail for his audiences. He shares his experiences; strategies; tactics and the many lessons learned over the years as an acquisition executive, investor and commercial real estate broker.

He enjoys training others about how to properly conduct the due diligence process when purchasing investment properties. The positive feedback he has received from investors, brokers and other commercial real estate professionals makes it very gratifying. He also believes it helps to raise the bar and standards for those professionals who assist others in buying commercial properties as they become more valuable team members and true allies to their clients.

You can reach him at brian@impactcoachingsystems.com.

The How to Add Value Handbook For Commercial Real Estate*

by Brian Hennessey

Quit running your investment property under the influence of "hopeium"; that delusional state under which you believe everything will work out fine without putting forth any effort or thought into creating value with it. That's the way most investors approach their investment property management plan.

Without a strategy for increasing value with your property's management plan is just taking the "lottery" approach.

You want the "Cliff Notes" version. In other words, the 20% that will give you 80% of the results, and not a bunch of minutia with 30 to 50 pages of fluff that you have to sift through to find the helpful tips or key points.

The fundamentals remain the same for the most part, when it comes to adding value and leasing. This information can be used across the various genres of commercial real estate investments, whether it's office and industrial, retail or multi-family residential properties. I comment from time to time throughout the book on the different angles or strategies you may want to consider for the different property types, which I have obtained from my own background and experience of 30+ years in the commercial real estate industry--or from those I know to be the best at their particular specialty.

In this handbook you will learn:

- How to determine the best way to price the rental rate for your investment property to get it leased at the highest value
- Find ways to make your property attractive to tenants
- How to interview and choose the right people that will help you get your property leased
- How to structure your lease rate and terms to create the most value for your investment property
- How to incentivize tenants to get your property leased in a down or over crowded market
- Strategies and tips to create more value
- Essential analysis forms, proposal and lease form samples, tenant application and other forms

These are very learnable skills that can be put into use right away to enhance your efforts to add value to your real estate investment. Well worth the time spent learning and implementing them.

I also spent time as a Vice President of Leasing for an investor who owned about 12 million square feet across the U.S, where I had to learn local practices and customs, as well as the ins-and-outs of the various markets such as Los Angeles, Dallas, Houston, Chicago, Orlando and Phoenix. Experiences learned during this phase of my career have also contributed to the contents of this book.

By learning and implementing these essential value-enhancing principles you can easily increase your property's cash flow exponentially. Every day you wait is another day of flushing more money down the drain. Buy it today and start generating more income, instead of hoping it all will work out. You will look back and consider it as one of your best real estate investments. Also available as an audiobook on Audible.com and iTunes.

"Brian Hennessey's books are invaluable staples, for both beginner and veteran alike. In his newest book, Brian again draws on his impressive experience to identify foundational best practices, developed from years in the trenches, and presented in a clear and concise format, creating another must-read, handbook that is, at the same time, both simple and smart."

– Robert McBride, Commercial Real Estate Broker

"This book has a wealth of information that is beneficial for all real estate professionals and owners. We are in the property management business and more and more owners today expect us to operate as asset managers with an eye for creating value for their respective properties. Many of the key elements to creating value through marketing, leasing, tenant mix and the right personnel for each property are included in the book. This is a must read and on-going resource for all who want to make money in the real estate business."

– Jock Ebner, President, Morlin Asset Management, LP

"As a 'value-add' player since the 1970's, I always look for ways to find opportunities in real estate. Whenever lucky enough to find something interesting, then the fun starts. Brian Hennessey's writing can help with that part, both for the seasoned veteran and the novice rookie. He goes into every area I could think of, and even some I have never thought of. A must-read for anyone wanting to make money as a principal real estate player."

– Maury Fagan, Real Estate Investor

"I've been a commercial real estate broker over three decades. After reading The How to Add Value Handbook For Commercial Real Estate, I believe it is as valuable as Brian Hennessey's book *"The Due Diligence Handbook For Commercial Real Estate"*; which I am still referring to so I can be certain that I am not missing anything while conducting due diligence. They contain so much valuable information, it is practically a "FOUND TREASURE" for anyone involved in commercial real estate, whether a seasoned realtor/broker or an investor/commercial property owner."

– Krich Adary, Director, Archetype Commercial Realty

The How To Add Value Handbook For Commercial Real Estate offers an in-the-trenches view of creating value in the real estate market. It's grounded, real world examples underscore the importance of thinking through design and leasing decisions with the end in mind.

– William King, AIA Architecture-Planning-Design

The Due Diligence Video Course for Commercial Real Estate and Certification Program

Thanks for purchasing and reading **The Due Diligence Handbook for Commercial Real Estate**. I'm sure you found some helpful tips and strategies to more competently and confidently deal with your investigation of investment properties and learned how you can *failure-proof* the commercial real estate opportunities you're looking to invest in. Once you understand how these are implemented and start using them to your advantage, I promise, you will not look at investing in them the same way *ever again*.

For some investors, after reading, they realize:

They need someone with experience who can help them through setting up their due diligence and walking them through their first transaction to help make it profitable and avoid as much risk as they possibly can, which I offer as a consultant.

Or

They may want to learn more about conducting the *deep dive* principles of due diligence with more *hands-on* instruction and material aids that makes the learning experience more inclusive, experiential and real.

The Due Diligence Video Course for Commercial Real Estate is a video course I've created, helping investors and real estate professionals learn the deep dive principles of conducting due diligence to help *failure-proof* their real estate investments so they can invest with *absolute confidence*.

It is jam-packed with the critical information you need and the essential tools, tips and strategies that you can use *immediately* while investing in commercial properties. This arsenal of information will make you *bullet proof* when you're investing in *any type* of real estate.

In it you'll find:

- 16 video modules that average 8-15 minutes in length and covers the essential information needed to make informed and intelligent decisions when investing
- Step-by-step instructions on what to do, what and who to ask to optimize uncovering a 'gold mine' of information to create value and save money
- A mock tenant interview to show you exactly what to ask of a tenant to help uncover critical information about a property you're looking to invest in
- Transcripts of each module to review later
- Copies of essential checklists, forms, sample lease proposals and Letters of Intent, Lease Comparable and Sale Comparable survey forms to help streamline your investing efforts, and much more
- Action Items list after each video module to get you into action right away and start implementing and internalizing the information you're learning
- A video of a walk-through inspection of a property pointing out highlighted areas of what to look out for
- How to properly underwrite the financial analysis throughout the entire due diligence process, so you can accurately assess the true value of the investment and successfully further negotiate a favorable discount with the seller

These are just some of the lessons and tools you'll acquire with the course. There is so much to know and learn about conducting deep dive due diligence and protecting yourself when purchasing investment property. The course offers you another way to embed this critical and essential information, so you can be a more competent and confident investor. You'll know *beyond a shadow of doubt* whether to move forward with an investment opportunity, *or not*, once you've completed it. You'll be *miles ahead* of most investors with this knowledge.

This course will pay for itself *exponentially* and *shave years* off your learning curve. I'm sharing with you all my hard-earned lessons and costly mistakes, so you don't have to learn them the hard way like I did while purchasing 9 million square feet of properties. It's also at a fraction of the cost that some of these mistakes cost me, without any of the headaches, humiliation and heartaches that I experienced.

The low hanging fruit has been picked in today's commercial real estate market. Don't pass on opportunities that don't have the obvious things many investors are looking for, like under market rents or big vacancies. This course will teach you where to find those *value enhancers* that most investors will miss or not even know where and what to look for.

Go to http://ImpactCoachingSystems.com/courses to check out the course.

For a **20% discount use the code DDHB20** upon checkout.

BONUS for real estate professionals:

If you're a real estate professional, there's an exam available at the end of the course where you can earn a Certificate of Completion upon successfully passing with a 70% or better pass rate. You can then download a copy of the certificate and a digital badge that can be placed on LinkedIn or another website you'd like to display it on. It shows others that you completed the course and are a **"Certified Investment Real Estate Acquisition and Due Diligence Specialist"**. This is a game-changer and a unique selling proposition that few agents offer, to help differentiate yourself from your competition.

I just want to say thanks again. Be sure to keep your eyes open for more valuable courses and information we offer at **impactcoachingsystems.com**, such as **The How to Add Value to Commercial Real Estate Video Course**. We have a lot more knowledge to share with you.

Course Guarantee

My 100% MONEY BACK GUARANTEE. NO QUESTIONS ASKED is good for 60 DAYS, that's 2 months from the time of your purchase.

Make sure you go to http://ImpactCoachingSystems.com/courses to check out the course today... you absolutely want this knowledge in your tool kit BEFORE you start considering your next deal.

Don't forget your 20% discount that we give as a thank you for reading this book. **Use the code DDHB20** upon checkout.

Made in the USA
Middletown, DE
28 December 2020